The Poetry of Edmund Waller

Volume II

Edmund Waller, FRS was born on March 3rd, 1606 in Coleshill, Buckinghamshire.

Waller was educated at the Royal Grammar School, High Wycombe and thence on to Eton and King's College, Cambridge. His adult life is very colourful and displays a man whose adventures and experiences made poetry an obvious vessel to express the journey.

He entered Parliament early, at age 18, and was, at first, an active member of the opposition. (Waller was to sit in Parliament at various times from 1624-1679) In 1631 he married a London heiress, a surreptitious marriage to a wealthy ward of the Court of Aldermen. Waller was brought before the Star Chamber for this offence, and heavily fined. Waller was however, a wealthy man and stayed so throughout his life despite the many fines he became liable for.

His wife bore him a son and a daughter at Beaconsfield but died in 1634.

After her death he unsuccessfully courted Lady Dorothy Sidney, the 'Sacharissa' of his poems.

By 1643 he had now switched sides to the Royalists and was the leader in the plot to seize London for Charles I, which is known as "Waller's Plot". On 30 May he and his friends were arrested. In the terror of discovery, Waller confessed "whatever he had said heard, thought or seen, and all that he knew... or suspected of others". His fellow conspirators were far braver and were unwilling to betray their principles or each other.

Waller was called before the bar of the House in July, and made an abject and complete speech of recantation. His life was spared and he was committed to the Tower of London, but, on paying a fine of £10,000, he was released and banished from the realm in November 1643.

It was now, in 1644 that he married Mary Bracey and together they took up residence at Rouen. She went on to bear him several children.

In 1646 Waller travelled with John Evelyn to Switzerland and Italy.

He made his peace with Cromwell in 1651 and returned to England but was only restored to favour with Cromwell's death and the Restoration of Charles II.

By now experience had taught him to keep all sides happy. Accordingly as he wrote poetic tributes to both Oliver Cromwell (1655) and Charles II (1660).

A precocious poet; he began to write, it is thought, in his late teens with a complimentary piece on His Majesty's Escape at St Andere written using the heroic couplet. Interestingly throughout his writing career he rejected the dense and intellectual verse of Metaphysical poetry. His more relaxed style helped prepare the way for the emergence of the heroic couplet. By the end of the 17th century it had become the dominant form of English poetry. His style is beguiling and of a polished simplicity. The great John Dryden thought him, along with Sir John Denham, as poets who brought about the Augustan age.

Edmund Waller died on October 21ˢᵗ, 1687 at the age of 81. He is buried at St Mary and All Saints Church, Beaconsfield

Index of Contents

OF HER MAJESTY, ON NEW-YEAR'S DAY, 1683

What revolutions in the world have been,
How are we changed since we first saw the Queen!
She, like the sun, does still the same appear,
Bright as she was at her arrival here!
Time has commission mortals to impair,
But things celestial is obliged to spare.

May every new year find her still the same
In health and beauty as she hither came!
When Lords and Commons, with united voice,
Th' Infanta named, approved the royal choice;[1]
First of our Queens whom not the King alone,
But the whole nation, lifted to the throne.

With like consent, and like desert, was crown'd
The glorious Prince[2] that does the Turk confound.
Victorious both! his conduct wins the day,
And her example chases vice away;
Though louder fame attend the martial rage,
'Tis greater glory to reform the age.

FOOTNOTES
[1] 'Royal choice': a royal message, announcing the king's intention to marry the Infanta of Portugal, was delivered in Parliament in May 1661.
[2] 'Prince': John Sobieski, king of Poland.

OF TEA, COMMENDED BY HER MAJESTY

Venus her myrtle, Phoebus has his bays;
Tea both excels, which she vouchsafes to praise.
The best of Queens, and best of herbs, we owe
To that bold nation which the way did show
To the fair region where the sun does rise,
Whose rich productions we so justly prize.
The Muse's friend, tea does our fancy aid,

Repress those vapours which the head invade,
And keeps that palace of the soul serene,
Fit on her birth-day to salute the Queen.

OF THE INVASION AND DEFEAT OF THE TURKS, IN THE YEAR 1683.[1]

The modern Nimrod, with a safe delight
Pursuing beasts, that save themselves by flight,
Grown proud, and weary of his wonted game,
Would Christians chase, and sacrifice to fame.

A prince, with eunuchs and the softer sex
Shut up so long, would warlike nations vex,
Provoke the German, and, neglecting heaven,
Forget the truce for which his oath was given.

His Grand Vizier, presuming to invest
The chief imperial city of the west,
With the first charge compell'd in haste to rise,
His treasure, tents, and cannon, left a prize;
The standard lost, and janizaries slain,
Render the hopes he gave his master vain.
The flying Turks, that bring the tidings home,
Renew the memory of his father's doom;
And his guard murmurs, that so often brings
Down from the throne their unsuccessful kings.

The trembling Sultan's forced to expiate
His own ill-conduct by another's fate.
The Grand Vizier, a tyrant, though a slave,
A fair example to his master gave;
He Bassa's head, to save his own, made fly,
And now, the Sultan to preserve, must die.

The fatal bowstring was not in his thought,
When, breaking truce, he so unjustly fought;
Made the world tremble with a numerous host,
And of undoubted victory did boast.

Strangled he lies! yet seems to cry aloud,
To warn the mighty, and instruct the proud,
That of the great, neglecting to be just,
Heaven in a moment makes a heap of dust.

The Turks so low, why should the Christians lose
Such an advantage of their barb'rous foes?

Neglect their present ruin to complete,
Before another Solyman they get?
Too late they would with shame, repenting, dread
That numerous herd, by such a lion led;
He Rhodes and Buda from the Christians tore,
Which timely union might again restore.

But, sparing Turks, as if with rage possess'd,
The Christians perish, by themselves oppress'd;
Cities and provinces so dearly won,
That the victorious people are undone!

What angel shall descend to reconcile
The Christian states, and end their guilty toil?
A prince more fit from heaven we cannot ask
Than Britain's king, for such a glorious task;
His dreadful navy, and his lovely mind,
Give him the fear and favour of mankind;
His warrant does the Christian faith defend;
On that relying, all their quarrels end.
The peace is sign'd,[2] and Britain does obtain
What Rome had sought from her fierce sons in vain.

In battles won Fortune a part doth claim,
And soldiers have their portion in the same;
In this successful union we find
Only the triumph of a worthy mind.
'Tis all accomplish'd by his royal word,
Without unsheathing the destructive sword;

Without a tax upon his subjects laid,
Their peace disturb'd, their plenty, or their trade.
And what can they to such a prince deny,
With whose desires the greatest kings comply?

The arts of peace are not to him unknown;
This happy way he march'd into the throne;
And we owe more to Heaven than to the sword,
The wish'd return of so benign a lord.

Charles! by old Greece with a new freedom graced,
Above her antique heroes shall be placed.
What Theseus did, or Theban Hercules,
Holds no compare with this victorious peace,
Which on the Turks shall greater honour gain,
Than all their giants and their monsters slain:
Those are bold tales, in fabulous ages told;
This glorious act the living do behold.

FOOTNOTES
[1] 'Year 1683': see History.
[2] 'Peace is signed': the Peace of Nimeguen.

A PRESAGE OF THE RUIN OF THE TURKISH EMPIRE; PRESENTED TO HIS MAJESTY KING JAMES II. ON HIS BIRTHDAY

Since James the Second graced the British throne,
Truce, well observed, has been infring'd by none;
Christians to him their present union owe,
And late success against the common foe;
While neighb'ring princes, both to urge their fate,
Court his assistance, and suspend their hate.
So angry bulls the combat do forbear,
When from the wood a lion does appear.

This happy day peace to our island sent,
As now he gives it to the Continent.
A prince more fit for such a glorious task,
Than England's king, from Heaven we cannot ask;
He, great and good! proportion'd to the work,
Their ill-drawn swords shall turn against the Turk.

Such kings, like stars with influence unconfined,
Shine with aspect propitious to mankind;
Favour the innocent, repress the bold,
And, while they flourish, make an age of gold.

Bred in the camp, famed for his valour, young;
At sea successful, vigorous, and strong;
His fleet, his array, and his mighty mind,
Esteem and rev'rence through the world do find.
A prince with such advantages as these,
Where he persuades not, may command a peace.
Britain declaring for the juster side,
The most ambitious will forget their pride;
They that complain will their endeavours cease,
Advised by him, inclined to present peace,
Join to the Turk's destruction, and then bring
All their pretences to so just a king.

If the successful troublers of mankind,
With laurel crown'd, so great applause do find,
Shall the vex'd world less honour yield to those
That stop their progress, and their rage oppose?

Next to that power which does the ocean awe,
Is to set bounds, and give ambition law.

The British monarch shall the glory have,
That famous Greece remains no longer slave;
That source of art and cultivated thought!
Which they to Rome, and Romans hither brought.

The banish'd Muses shall no longer mourn,
But may with liberty to Greece return;
Though slaves (like birds that sing not in a cage),
They lost their genius, and poetic rage;
Homers again, and Pindars, may be found,
And his great actions with their numbers crown'd.

The Turk's vast empire does united stand;
Christians, divided under the command
Of jarring princes, would be soon undone,
Did not this hero make their int'rest one;
Peace to embrace, ruin the common foe,
Exalt the Cross, and lay the Crescent low.

Thus may the Gospel to the rising sun
Be spread, and flourish where it first began;
And this great day, (so justly honour'd here!)
Known to the East, and celebrated there.

Hæc ego longævus cecini tibi, maxime regum!
Ausus et ipse manu juvenum tentare laborem.—VIRG.

EPISTLES

TO THE KING, ON HIS NAVY

Where'er thy navy spreads her canvas wings,
Homage to thee, and peace to all she brings;
The French and Spaniard, when thy flags appear,
Forget their hatred, and consent to fear.
So Jove from Ida did both hosts survey,
And when he pleased to thunder, part the fray.
Ships heretofore in seas like fishes sped,
The mightiest still upon the smallest fed;
Thou on the deep imposest nobler laws,
And by that justice hast removed the cause
Of those rude tempests, which for rapine sent,
Too oft, alas! involved the innocent.

Now shall the ocean, as thy Thames, be free
From both those fates, of storms and piracy.

But we most happy, who can fear no force
But winged troops, or Pegasean horse.
'Tis not so hard for greedy foes to spoil
Another nation, as to touch our soil.
Should Nature's self invade the world again,
And o'er the centre spread the liquid main,
Thy power were safe, and her destructive hand
Would but enlarge the bounds of thy command;
Thy dreadful fleet would style thee lord of all,
And ride in triumph o'er the drowned ball;
Those towers of oak o'er fertile plains might go,
And visit mountains where they once did grow.

The world's Restorer once could not endure
That finish'd Babel should those men secure,
Whose pride design'd that fabric to have stood
Above the reach of any second flood;
To thee, his chosen, more indulgent, he
Dares trust such power with so much piety.

TO MR HENRY LAWES,[1] WHO HAD THEN NEWLY SET A SONG OF MINE IN THE YEAR 1635

Verse makes heroic virtue live;
But you can life to verses give.
As when in open air we blow,
The breath, though strain'd, sounds flat and low;
But if a trumpet take the blast,
It lifts it high, and makes it last:
So in your airs our numbers dress'd,
Make a shrill sally from the breast
Of nymphs, who, singing what we penn'd,
Our passions to themselves commend;
While love, victorious with thy art,
Governs at once their voice and heart.

You by the help of tune and time,
Can make that song that was but rhyme.
Noy[2] pleading, no man doubts the cause;
Or questions verses set by Lawes.

As a church window, thick with paint,
Lets in a light but dim and faint;
So others, with division, hide

The light of sense, the poet's pride:
But you alone may proudly boast
That not a syllable is lost;
The writer's and the setter's skill
At once the ravish'd ears do fill.
Let those which only warble long,
And gargle in their throats a song,
Content themselves with Ut, Re, Mi:[3]
Let words, and sense, be set by thee.

FOOTNOTES

[1] 'Lawes': an eminent musical composer, who composed the music for Milton's Comus.
[2] 'Noy': Attorney-General to Charles I., had died in 1635. By a poetical licence Waller represents him still pleading.
[3] 'Ut, Re, Mi': Lawes opposed the Italian music.

THE COUNTRY TO MY LADY CARLISLE.[1]

I

Madam, of all the sacred Muse inspired,
Orpheus alone could with the woods comply;
Their rude inhabitants his song admired,
And Nature's self, in those that could not lie:
Your beauty next our solitude invades,
And warms us, shining through the thickest shades.

II

Nor ought the tribute, which the wond'ring Court
Pays your fair eyes, prevail with you to scorn
The answer and consent to that report
Which, echo-like, the country does return:
Mirrors are taught to flatter, but our springs
Present th'impartial images of things.

III

A rural judge disposed of beauty's prize;
A simple shepherd was preferr'd to Jove;
Down to the mountains from the partial skies,
Came Juno, Pallas, and the Queen of Love,
To plead for that which was so justly given
To the bright Carlisle of the court of heaven.

IV

Carlisle! a name which all our woods are taught,
Loud as their Amaryllis, to resound;
Carlisle! a name which on the bark is wrought

Of every tree that's worthy of the wound.
From Phoebus' rage our shadows and our streams
May guard us better than from Carlisle's beams.

FOOTNOTE
*[1] 'Lady Carlisle': the Lady Lucy Percy, daughter of the Earl of Northumberland, married against her
father's wishes to the Earl of Carlisle. She was a wit and intriguante.*

TO PHYLLIS

Phyllis! 'twas love that injured you,
And on that rock your Thrysis threw;
Who for proud Celia could have died,
While you no less accused his pride.

Fond Love his darts at random throws,
And nothing springs from what he sows;
From foes discharged, as often meet
The shining points of arrows fleet,
In the wide air creating fire,
As souls that join in one desire.

Love made the lovely Venus burn
In vain, and for the cold youth[1] mourn,
Who the pursuit of churlish beasts
Preferr'd to sleeping on her breasts.

Love makes so many hearts the prize
Of the bright Carlisle's conqu'ring eyes,
Which she regards no more than they
The tears of lesser beauties weigh.
So have I seen the lost clouds pour
Into the sea an useless shower;
And the vex'd sailors curse the rain
For which poor shepherds pray'd in vain.

Then, Phyllis, since our passions are
Govern'd by chance, and not the care,
But sport of heaven, which takes delight
To look upon this Parthian fight
Of love, still flying, or in chase,
Never encount'ring face to face;
No more to Love we'll sacrifice,
But to the best of deities;
And let our hearts, which Love disjoin'd,
By his kind mother be combin'd.

TO THE QUEEN-MOTHER OF FRANCE, UPON HER LANDING [1]

Great Queen of Europe! where thy offspring wears
All the chief crowns; where princes are thy heirs;
As welcome thou to sea-girt Britain's shore,
As erst Latona (who fair Cynthia bore)
To Delos was; here shines a nymph as bright,
By thee disclosed, with like increase of light.
Why was her joy in Belgia confined?
Or why did you so much regard the wind?
Scarce could the ocean, though enraged, have toss'd
Thy sov'reign bark, but where th'obsequious coast
Pays tribute to thy bed. Rome's conqu'ring hand
More vanquished nations under her command
Never reduced. Glad Berecynthia so
Among her deathless progeny did go;
A wreath of towers adorn'd her rev'rend head,
Mother of all that on ambrosia fed.
Thy godlike race must sway the age to come,
As she Olympus peopled with her womb.

Would those commanders of mankind obey
Their honour'd parent, all pretences lay
Down at your royal feet, compose their jars,
And on the growing Turk discharge these wars;
The Christian knights that sacred tomb should wrest
From Pagan hands, and triumph o'er the East;
Our England's Prince, and Gallia's Dolphin, might
Like young Rinaldo and Tancredi fight;
In single combat by their swords again
The proud Argantes and fierce Soldan slain;
Again might we their valiant deeds recite,
And with your Tuscan Muse[2] exalt the fight.

TO VANDYCK [1]

Rare Artisan, whose pencil moves
Not our delights alone, but loves!
From thy shop of beauty we
Slaves return, that enter'd free.
The heedless lover does not know
Whose eyes they are that wound him so;
But, confounded with thy art,
Inquires her name that has his heart.
Another, who did long refrain,
Feels his old wound bleed fresh again
With dear remembrance of that face,
Where now he reads new hope of grace:
Nor scorn nor cruelty does find,
But gladly suffers a false wind
To blow the ashes of despair
From the reviving brand of care.
Fool! that forgets her stubborn look
This softness from thy finger took.
Strange! that thy hand should not inspire
The beauty only, but the fire;
Not the form alone, and grace,
But act and power of a face.
Mayst thou yet thyself as well,
As all the world besides, excel!
So you th'unfeigned truth rehearse
(That I may make it live in verse),
Why thou couldst not at one assay,[2]
The face to aftertimes convey,
Which this admires. Was it thy wit
To make her oft before thee sit?
Confess, and we'll forgive thee this;
For who would not repeat that bliss,
And frequent sight of such a dame
Buy with the hazard of his fame?
Yet who can tax thy blameless skill,
Though thy good hand had failed still,
When Nature's self so often errs?
She for this many thousand years
Seems to have practised with much care,
To frame the race of women fair;
Yet never could a perfect birth
Produce before to grace the earth,
Which waxèd old ere it could see
Her that amazed thy art and thee.
But now 'tis done, oh, let me know
Where those immortal colours grow,

That could this deathless piece compose!
In lilies? or the fading rose?
No; for this theft thou hast climb'd higher
Than did Prometheus for his fire.

FOOTNOTES

[1] *'Vandyck': some think this refers to a picture of Saccharissa, by Vandyck, in Hall-Barn.*
[2] *'Assay': attempt.*

TO MY LORD OF LEICESTER [1]

I

Not that thy trees at Penshurst groan,
Oppressed with their timely load,
And seem to make their silent moan,
That their great lord is now abroad:
They to delight his taste, or eye,
Would spend themselves in fruit, and die.

II

Not that thy harmless deer repine,
And think themselves unjustly slain
By any other hand than thine,
Whose arrows they would gladly stain;
No, nor thy friends, which hold too dear
That peace with France which keeps thee there.

III

All these are less than that great cause
Which now exacts your presence here,
Wherein there meet the divers laws
Of public and domestic care.
For one bright nymph our youth contends,
And on your prudent choice depends.

IV

Not the bright shield of Thetis' son[2]
(For which such stern debate did rise,
That the great Ajax Telamon
Refused to live without the prize),
Those Achive peers did more engage
Than she the gallants of our age.

V

That beam of beauty, which begun
To warm us so when thou wert here,

Now scorches like the raging sun,
When Sirius does first appear.
Oh, fix this flame! and let despair
Redeem the rest from endless care.

FOOTNOTES

[1] 'Lord of Leicester': Saccharissa's father. He was employed at this time in foreign service.
[2] 'Thetis' son': Achilles.

TO MRS BRAUGHTON, SERVANT TO SACCHARISSA

Fair fellow-servant! may your gentle ear
Prove more propitious to my slighted care
Than the bright dame's we serve: for her relief
(Vex'd with the long expressions of my grief)
Receive these plaints; nor will her high disdain
Forbid my humble Muse to court her train.

So, in those nations which the sun adore,
Some modest Persian, or some weak-eyed Moor,
No higher dares advance his dazzled sight,
Than to some gilded cloud, which near the light
Of their ascending god adorns the east,
And, gracèd with his beams, outshines the rest.

Thy skilful hand contributes to our woe,
And whets those arrows which confound us so.
A thousand Cupids in those curls do sit
(Those curious nets!) thy slender fingers knit.
The Graces put not more exactly on
Th' attire of Venus, when the ball she won,
Than Saccharissa by thy care is dress'd,
When all our youth prefers her to the rest.

You the soft season know when best her mind
May be to pity, or to love, inclined:
In some well-chosen hour supply his fear,
Whose hopeless love durst never tempt the ear
Of that stern goddess. You, her priest, declare
What offerings may propitiate the fair;
Rich orient pearl, bright stones that ne'er decay,
Or polish'd lines, which longer last than they;
For if I thought she took delight in those,
To where the cheerful morn does first disclose,
(The shady night removing with her beams),
Wing'd with bold love, I'd fly to fetch such gems.

But since her eyes, her teeth, her lip excels
All that is found in mines or fishes' shells,
Her nobler part as far exceeding these,
None but immortal gifts her mind should please.
The shining jewels Greece and Troy bestow'd
On Sparta's queen,[1] her lovely neck did load,
And snowy wrists; but when the town was burn'd,
Those fading glories were to ashes turn'd;
Her beauty, too, had perished, and her fame,
Had not the Muse redeemed them from the flame.

FOOTNOTE
[1] 'Sparta's queen': Helen.

TO MY YOUNG LADY LUCY SIDNEY [1]

I
Why came I so untimely forth
Into a world which, wanting thee,
Could entertain us with no worth
Or shadow of felicity?
That time should me so far remove
From that which I was born to love!

II
Yet, fairest blossom! do not slight
That age which you may know so soon;
The rosy morn resigns her light
And milder glory to the noon;
And then what wonders shall you do,
Whose dawning beauty warms us so?

III
Hope waits upon the flow'ry prime;
And summer, though it be less gay,
Yet is not look'd on as a time
Of declination or decay;
For with a full hand that does bring
All that was promised by the spring.

FOOTNOTE
[1] 'Lady Lucy Sidney': the younger sister of Lady Dorothea; afterwards married to Sir John Pelham.

TO AMORET [1]

Fair! that you may truly know
What you unto Thyrsis owe,
I will tell you how I do
Saccharissa love and you.

Joy salutes me, when I set
My bless'd eyes on Amoret;
But with wonder I am strook,
While I on the other look.

If sweet Amoret complains,
I have sense of all her pains;
But for Saccharissa I
Do not only grieve, but die.

All that of myself is mine,
Lovely Amoret! is thine;
Saccharissa's captive fain
Would untie his iron chain,
And, those scorching beams to shun,
To thy gentle shadow run.

If the soul had free election
To dispose of her affection,
I would not thus long have borne
Haughty Saccharissa's scorn;
But 'tis sure some power above,
Which controls our wills in love!

If not love, a strong desire
To create and spread that fire
In my breast, solicits me,
Beauteous Amoret! for thee.

'Tis amazement more than love,
Which her radiant eyes do move;
If less splendour wait on thine,
Yet they so benignly shine,
I would turn my dazzled sight
To behold their milder light;
But as hard 'tis to destroy
That high flame, as to enjoy;
Which how eas'ly I may do,
Heaven (as eas'ly scaled) does know!

Amoret! as sweet and good
As the most delicious food,

Which, but tested, does impart
Life and gladness to the heart.

Saccharissa's beauty's wine,
Which to madness doth incline;
Such a liquor as no brain
That is mortal can sustain.

Scarce can I to heaven excuse
The devotion which I use
Unto that adorèd dame;
For 'tis not unlike the same
Which I thither ought to send;
So that if it could take end,
'Twould to heaven itself be due
To succeed her, and not you,
Who already have of me
All that's not idolatry;
Which, though not so fierce a flame,
Is longer like to be the same.

Then smile on me, and I will prove
Wonder is shorter-liv'd than love.

FOOTNOTE
[1] 'Amoret': see 'Life.'

TO MY LORD OF FALKLAND [1]

Brave Holland leads, and with him Falkland goes:
Who hears this told, and does not straight suppose
We send the Graces and the Muses forth
To civilise and to instruct the north?
Not that these ornaments make swords less sharp;
Apollo bears as well his bow as harp;[2]
And though he be the patron of that spring,
Where, in calm peace, the sacred virgins sing,
He courage had to guard th'invaded throne
Of Jove, and cast th'ambitious giants down.

Ah, noble friend! with what impatience all
That know thy worth, and know how prodigal
Of thy great soul thou art (longing to twist
Bays with that ivy which so early kiss'd
Thy youthful temples), with what horror we
Think on the blind events of war and thee!

To fate exposing that all-knowing breast
Among the throng, as cheaply as the rest;
Where oaks and brambles (if the copse be burn'd)
Confounded lie, to the same ashes turn'd.

Some happy wind over the ocean blow
This tempest yet, which frights our island so!
Guarded with ships, and all the sea our own,
From heaven this mischief on our heads is thrown.

In a late dream, the genius of this land,
Amazed, I saw, like the fair Hebrew, stand,
When first she felt the twins begin to jar,[3]
And found her womb the seat of civil war.
Inclined to whose relief, and with presage
Of better fortune for the present age,
Heaven sends, quoth I, this discord for our good,
To warm, perhaps, but not to waste our blood;
To raise our drooping spirits, grown the scorn
Of our proud neighbours, who ere long shall mourn
(Though now they joy in our expected harms)
We had occasion to resume our arms.

A lion so with self-provoking smart
(His rebel tail scourging his nobler part)
Calls up his courage; then begins to roar,
And charge his foes, who thought him mad before.

FOOTNOTES
[1] 'Lord of Falkland': referring to the unsuccessful expedition of Charles I. against Scotland in 1639,
frustrated by the cowardice or treachery of Lord Holland.
[2] 'Bow as harp': Horace, Ode iv., lib. 3.
[3] 'Twins begin to jar': Gen. xxv. 22.

TO MY LORD NORTHUMBERLAND, UPON THE DEATH OF HIS LADY [1]

To this great loss a sea of tears is due;
But the whole debt not to be paid by you.
Charge not yourself with all, nor render vain
Those show'rs the eyes of us your servants rain.
Shall grief contract the largeness of that heart,
In which nor fear, nor anger, has a part?
Virtue would blush if time should boast (which dries,
Her sole child dead, the tender mother's eyes)
Your mind's relief, where reason triumphs so
Over all passions, that they ne'er could grow

Beyond their limits in your noble breast,
To harm another, or impeach your rest.
This we observed, delighting to obey
One who did never from his great self stray;
Whose mild example seemed to engage
Th' obsequious seas, and teach them not to rage.

The brave Aemilius, his great charge laid down
(The force of Rome, and fate of Macedon),
In his lost sons did feel the cruel stroke
Of changing fortune, and thus highly spoke
Before Rome's people: 'We did oft implore,
That if the heavens had any bad in store
For your Aemilius, they would pour that ill
On his own house, and let you flourish still.'
You on the barren seas, my lord, have spent
Whole springs and summers to the public lent;
Suspended all the pleasures of your life,
And shorten'd the short joy of such a wife;
For which your country's more obligèd than
For many lives of old less happy men.
You, that have sacrificed so great a part
Of youth, and private bliss, ought to impart
Your sorrow too, and give your friends a right
As well in your affliction as delight.
Then with Aemilian courage bear this cross,
Since public persons only public loss
Ought to affect. And though her form and youth,
Her application to your will, and truth,
That noble sweetness, and that humble state
(All snatch'd away by such a hasty fate!)
Might give excuse to any common breast,
With the huge weight of so just grief oppress'd;
Yet let no portion of your life be stain'd
With passion, but your character maintain'd
To the last act. It is enough her stone
May honour'd be with superscription
Of the sole lady who had power to move
The great Northumberland to grieve, and love.

FOOTNOTE
*[1] 'His lady': the Lady Anne Cecil, daughter of the Earl of Salisbury.
See a previous note.*

TO MY LORD ADMIRAL, OF HIS LATE SICKNESS AND RECOVERY

With joy like ours the Thracian youth invades
Orpheus, returning from th'Elysian shades;
Embrace the hero, and his stay implore;
Make it their public suit he would no more
Desert them so, and for his spouse's sake,
His vanish'd love, tempt the Lethean lake.
The ladies, too, the brightest of that time
(Ambitious all his lofty bed to climb),
Their doubtful hopes with expectation feed,
Who shall the fair Eurydice succeed:
Eurydice! for whom his numerous moan
Makes list'ning trees and savage mountains groan;
Through all the air his sounding strings dilate
Sorrow, like that which touch'd our hearts of late.
Your pining sickness, and your restless pain,
At once the land affecting, and the main,
When the glad news that you were admiral
Scarce through the nation spread,[1] 'twas feared by all
That our great Charles, whose wisdom shines in you,
Would be perplexed how to choose anew.
So more than private was the joy and grief,
That at the worst it gave our souls relief,
That in our age such sense of virtue lived,
They joy'd so justly, and so justly grieved.
Nature (her fairest light eclipsèd) seems
Herself to suffer in those sharp extremes;
While not from thine alone thy blood retires,
But from those cheeks which all the world admires.
The stem thus threaten'd, and the sap in thee,
Droop all the branches of that noble tree!
Their beauty they, and we our love suspend;
Nought can our wishes, save thy health, intend.
As lilies overcharged with rain, they bend
Their beauteous heads, and with high heaven contend;
Fold thee within their snowy arms, and cry—
'He is too faultless, and too young, to die!'
So like immortals round about thee they
Sit, that they fright approaching death away.
Who would not languish, by so fair a train
To be lamented, and restored again?

Or, thus withheld, what hasty soul would go,
Though to the blest? O'er young Adonis so
Fair Venus mourn'd, and with the precious shower
Of her warm tears cherish'd the springing flower.

The next support, fair hope of your great name,
And second pillar of that noble frame,

By loss of thee would no advantage have,
But step by step pursue thee to the grave.

And now relentless Fate, about to end
The line which backward does so far extend
That antique stock, which still the world supplies
With bravest spirits, and with brightest eyes,
Kind Phoebus, interposing, bid me say,
Such storms no more shall shake that house; but they,
Like Neptune, and his sea-born niece,[1] shall be
The shining glories of the land and sea;
With courage guard, and beauty warm, our age,
And lovers fill with like poetic rage.

FOOTNOTE
[1] 'Nation spread': the Earl of Northumberland, appointed Lord High Admiral in the year 1638.

TO THE QUEEN, OCCASIONED UPON SIGHT OF HER MAJESTY'S PICTURE [2]

Well fare the hand, which to our humble sight
Presents that beauty, which the dazzling light
Of royal splendour hides from weaker eyes,
And all access, save by this art, denies.
Here only we have courage to behold
This beam of glory; here we dare unfold
In numbers thus the wonders we conceive;
The gracious image, seeming to give leave,
Propitious stands, vouchsafing to be seen;
And by our Muse saluted Mighty Queen,
In whom th'extremes of power and beauty move,
The Queen of Britain and the Queen of Love!

As the bright sun (to which we owe no sight
Of equal glory to your beauty's light)
Is wisely placed in so sublime a seat,
T' extend his light, and moderate his heat;
So, happy 'tis you move in such a sphere,
As your high Majesty with awful fear
In human breasts might qualify that fire,
Which, kindled by those eyes, had flamèd higher
Than when the scorched world like hazard run,
By the approach of the ill-guided sun.

No other nymphs have title to men's hearts,
But as their meanness larger hope imparts;
Your beauty more the fondest lover moves

With admiration than his private loves;
With admiration! for a pitch so high
(Save sacred Charles his) never love durst fly.
Heaven, that preferr'd a sceptre to your hand,
Favour'd our freedom more than your command;
Beauty had crown'd you, and you must have been
The whole world's mistress, other than a Queen.
All had been rivals, and you might have spared,
Or kill'd, and tyrannised, without a guard;
No power achieved, either by arms or birth,
Equals love's empire both in heaven and earth.
Such eyes as yours on Jove himself have thrown
As bright and fierce a lightning as his own;
Witness our Jove, prevented by their flame
In his swift passage to th'Hesperian dame;

When, like a lion, finding, in his way
To some intended spoil, a fairer prey,
The royal youth pursuing the report
Of beauty, found it in the Gallic court;
There public care with private passion fought
A doubtful combat in his noble thought:
Should he confess his greatness, and his love,
And the free faith of your great brother[3] prove;
With his Achates breaking through the cloud
Of that disguise which did their graces shroud;[4]
And mixing with those gallants at the ball,
Dance with the ladies, and outshine them all;
Or on his journey o'er the mountains ride?—
So when the fair Leucothoë he espied,
To check his steeds impatient Phoebus yearn'd,
Though all the world was in his course concern'd.
What may hereafter her meridian do,
Whose dawning beauty warm'd his bosom so?
Not so divine a flame, since deathless gods
Forbore to visit the defiled abodes
Of men, in any mortal breast did burn;
Nor shall, till piety and they return.

FOOTNOTES
[1] 'Sea-born niece': Venus.
[2] 'Majesty's picture': Henrietta, daughter of Henry IV., married by proxy to Charles I. in Paris, 1st May
1625. Marriages made in May are said to be unlucky—this certainly was.
[3] 'Great brother': Louis XIII., King of France.
[4] 'Graces shroud': 'Achates,' the Duke of Buckingham.

TO AMORET

I
Amoret! the Milky Way
Framed of many nameless stars!
The smooth stream where none can say
He this drop to that prefers!

II
Amoret! my lovely foe!
Tell me where thy strength does lie?
Where the pow'r that charms us so?
In thy soul, or in thy eye?

III
By that snowy neck alone,
Or thy grace in motion seen,
No such wonders could he done;
Yet thy waist is straight and clean
As Cupid's shaft, or Hermes' rod,
And pow'rful, too, as either god.

TO PHYLLIS

Phyllis! why should we delay
Pleasures shorter than the day?
Could we (which we never can!)
Stretch our lives beyond their span,
Beauty like a shadow flies,
And our youth before us dies.
Or would youth and beauty stay,
Love hath wings, and will away.
Love hath swifter wings than Time,
Change in love to heaven does climb.
Gods, that never change their state,
Vary oft their love and hate.

Phyllis! to this truth we owe
All the love betwixt us two.
Let not you and I inquire
What has been our past desire;
On what shepherds you have smiled,
Or what nymphs I have beguiled;
Leave it to the planets too,
What we shall hereafter do;

For the joys we now may prove,
Take advice of present love.

TO SIR WILLIAM DAVENANT, UPON HIS TWO FIRST BOOKS OF GONDIBERT.[1] WRITTEN IN FRANCE

Thus the wise nightingale that leaves her home,
Her native wood, when storms and winter come,
Pursuing constantly the cheerful spring,
To foreign groves does her old music bring.

The drooping Hebrews' banish'd harps, unstrung,
At Babylon upon the willows hung;
Yours sounds aloud, and tells us you excel
No less in courage, than in singing well;
While, unconcern'd, you let your country know
They have impoverish'd themselves, not you;
Who, with the Muses' help, can mock those fates
Which threaten kingdoms, and disorder states.
So Ovid, when from Cæsar's rage he fled,
The Roman Muse to Pontus with him led;
Where he so sung, that we, through pity's glass,
See Nero milder than Augustus was.
Hereafter such, in thy behalf, shall be
Th' indulgent censure of posterity.
To banish those who with such art can sing,
Is a rude crime, which its own curse doth bring;
Ages to come shall ne'er know how they fought,
Nor how to love, their present youth be taught.

This to thyself.—Now to thy matchless book,
Wherein those few that can with judgment look,
May find old love in pure fresh language told,
Like new-stamp'd coin made out of angel-gold.
Such truth in love as th'antique world did know,
In such a style as courts may boast of now;
Which no bold tales of gods or monsters swell,
But human passions, such as with us dwell.
Man is thy theme; his virtue or his rage
Drawn to the life in each elaborate page.
Mars nor Bellona are not namèd here,
But such a Gondibert as both might fear;
Venus had here, and Hebe, been outshined
By the bright Birtha and thy Rhodalind.
Such is thy happy skill, and such the odds
Betwixt thy worthies and the Grecian gods!
Whose deities in vain had here come down,

Where mortal beauty wears the Sovereign crown;
Such as of flesh compos'd, by flesh and blood,
Though not resisted, may be understood.

FOOTNOTE

[1] 'Sir William Davenant': Davenant fled to France in fear of the displeasure of the Parliament, and there
wrote the two first cantos of Gondibert.

TO MY WORTHY FRIEND, MR WASE, THE TRANSLATOR OF GRATIUS [1]

I
Thus, by the music, we may know
When noble wits a-hunting go,
Through groves that on Parnassus grow.

II
The Muses all the chase adorn;
My friend on Pegasus is borne;
And young Apollo winds the horn.

III
Having old Gratius in the wind,
No pack of critics e'er could find,
Or he know more of his own mind.

IV
Here huntsmen with delight may read
How to choose dogs for scent or speed,
And how to change or mend the breed;

V
What arms to use, or nets to frame,
Wild beasts to combat or to tame;
With all the myst'ries of that game.

VI
But, worthy friend! the face of war
In ancient times doth differ far
From what our fiery battles are.

VII
Nor is it like, since powder known,
That man, so cruel to his own,
Should spare the race of beasts alone.

VIII
No quarter now, but with the gun

Men wait in trees from sun to sun,
And all is in a moment done.

IX
And therefore we expect your next
Should be no comment, but a text
To tell how modern beasts are vex'd.

X
Thus would I further yet engage
Your gentle Muse to court the age
With somewhat of your proper rage;

XI
Since none does more to Phoebus owe,
Or in more languages can show
Those arts which you so early know.

FOOTNOTE
[1] 'Mr. Wase': Wase was a fellow of Cambridge, tutor to Lord Herbert, and translator of Grathis on
'Hunting,' a very learned man.

TO A FRIEND, ON THE DIFFERENT SUCCESS OF THEIR LOVES [1]

Thrice happy pair! of whom we cannot know
Which first began to love, or loves most now;
Fair course of passion! where two lovers start,
And run together, heart still yoked with heart;
Successful youth! whom love has taught the way
To be victorious in the first essay.
Sure love's an art best practisèd at first,
And where th'experienced still prosper worst!
I, with a different fate, pursued in vain
The haughty Cælia, till my just disdain
Of her neglect, above that passion borne,
Did pride to pride oppose, and scorn to scorn.
Now she relents; but all too late to move
A heart directed to a nobler love.
The scales are turn'd, her kindness weighs no more
Now, than my vows and service did before.
So in some well-wrought hangings you may see
How Hector leads, and how the Grecians flee;
Here, the fierce Mars his courage so inspires,
That with bold hands the Argive fleet he fires;
But there, from heaven the blue-eyed virgin[2] falls,
And frighted Troy retires within her walls;

They that are foremost in that bloody race,
Turn head anon, and give the conqu'rors chase.
So like the chances are of love and war,
That they alone in this distinguish'd are,
In love the victors from the vanquish'd fly;
They fly that wound, and they pursue that die.

FOOTNOTES

[1] 'Their loves': supposed to be Alexander Hampden, involved with Waller in the plot. See 'Life'
[2] 'Blue-eyed virgin': Minerva.

TO ZELINDA [1]

Fairest piece of well-form'd earth!
Urge not thus your haughty birth;
The power which you have o'er us lies
Not in your race, but in your eyes.
'None but a prince!'—Alas! that voice
Confines you to a narrow choice.
Should you no honey vow to taste,
But what the master-bees have placed
In compass of their cells, how small
A portion to your share would fall!
Nor all appear, among those few,
Worthy the stock from whence they grew.
The sap which at the root is bred
In trees, through all the boughs is spread;
But virtues which in parents shine,
Make not like progress through the line.
'Tis not from whom, but where, we live;
The place does oft those graces give.
Great Julius, on the mountains bred,
A flock perhaps, or herd, had led.
He that the world subdued,[2] had been
But the best wrestler on the green.
'Tis art and knowledge which draw forth
The hidden seeds of native worth;
They blow those sparks, and make them rise
Into such flames as touch the skies.
To the old heroes hence was given
A pedigree which reached to heaven;
Of mortal seed they were not held,
Which other mortals so excell'd.
And beauty, too, in such excess
As yours, Zelinda! claims no less.
Smile but on me, and you shall scorn,

Henceforth, to be of princes born.
I can describe, the shady grove
Where your loved mother slept with Jove;
And yet excuse the faultless dame,
Caught with her spouse's shape and name.
Thy matchless form will credit bring
To all the wonders I shall sing.

FOOTNOTES

[1] 'Zelinda': referring to a novel where the lady, a princess, refuses a lover, saying, 'I will have none but a prince!'
[2] 'World subdued': Alexander.

TO MY LADY MORTON, ON NEW-YEAR'S DAY,[1] AT THE LOUVRE IN PARIS.

Madam! new years may well expect to find
Welcome from you, to whom they are so kind;
Still as they pass, they court and smile on you,
And make your beauty, as themselves, seem new.
To the fair Villiers we Dalkeith prefer,
And fairest Morton now as much to her;
So like the sun's advance your titles show,
Which as he rises does the warmer grow.

But thus to style you fair, your sex's praise,
Gives you but myrtle, who may challenge bays;
From armed foes to bring a royal prize,
Shows your brave heart victorious as your eyes.
If Judith, marching with the gen'ral's head,
Can give us passion when her story's read,
What may the living do, which brought away,
Though a less bloody, yet a nobler prey;
Who from our flaming Troy, with a bold hand,
Snatch'd her fair charge, the Princess, like a brand?
A brand! preserved to warm some prince's heart,
And make whole kingdoms take her brother's part.
So Venus, from prevailing Greeks, did shroud
The hope of Rome, and saved him in a cloud.

This gallant act may cancel all our rage,
Begin a better, and absolve this age.
Dark shades become the portrait of our time;
Here weeps Misfortune, and there triumphs Crime!
Let him that draws it hide the rest in night;
This portion only may endure the light,
Where the kind nymph, changing her faultless shape,

Becomes unhandsome, handsomely to 'scape,
When through the guards, the river, and the sea,
Faith, beauty, wit, and courage, made their way.
As the brave eagle does with sorrow see
The forest wasted, and that lofty tree
Which holds her nest about to be o'erthrown,
Before the feathers of her young are grown,
She will not leave them, nor she cannot stay,
But bears them boldly on her wings away;
So fled the dame, and o'er the ocean bore
Her princely burthen to the Gallic shore.
Born in the storms of war, this royal fair,
Produced like lightning in tempestuous air,
Though now she flies her native isle (less kind,
Less safe for her than either sea or wind!)
Shall, when the blossom of her beauty's blown,
See her great brother on the British throne;
Where peace shall smile, and no dispute arise,
But which rules most, his sceptre, or her eyes.

FOOTNOTE

[1] 'New-year's day': Lady Morton, daughter of Sir Edward Villiers, niece of the Duke of Buckingham, and wife of Lord Douglas, of Dalkeith, one of the most celebrated beauties of her day. She accompanied the Princess Henrietta in disguise to Paris. Waller, then in France, wrote these lines in 1650.

TO A FAIR LADY, PLAYING WITH A SNAKE

I
Strange! that such horror and such grace
Should dwell together in one place;
A fury's arm, an angel's face!

II
'Tis innocence, and youth, which makes
In Chloris' fancy such mistakes,
To start at love, and play with snakes.

III
By this and by her coldness barr'd,
Her servants have a task too hard;
The tyrant has a double guard!

IV
Thrice happy snake! that in her sleeve
May boldly creep; we dare not give
Our thoughts so unconfined a leave.

V

Contented in that nest of snow
He lies, as he his bliss did know,
And to the wood no more would go.

Vi

Take heed, fair Eve! you do not make
Another tempter of this snake;
A marble one so warm'd would speak.

TO HIS WORTHY FRIEND MASTER EVELYN,[1] UPON HIS TRANSLATION OF 'LUCRETIUS.'

Lucretius, (with a stork-like fate,
Born, and translated, in a state)
Comes to proclaim, in English verse,
No Monarch rules the universe;
But chance, and atoms, make this All
In order democratical,
Where bodies freely run their course,
Without design, or fate, or force.
And this in such a strain he sings,
As if his Muse, with angels' wings,
Had soar'd beyond our utmost sphere,
And other worlds discover'd there;
For his immortal, boundless wit,
To Nature does no bounds permit,
But boldly has removed those bars
Of heaven, and earth, and seas, and stars,
By which they were before supposed,
By narrow wits, to be enclosed,
Till his free Muse threw down the pale,
And did at once dispark them all.

So vast this argument did seem,
That the wise author did esteem
The Roman language (which was spread
O'er the whole world, in triumph led)
A tongue too narrow to unfold
The wonders which he would have told.
This speaks thy glory, noble friend!
And British language does commend;
For here Lucretius whole we find,
His words, his music, and his mind.
Thy art has to our country brought
All that he writ, and all he thought.

Ovid translated, Virgil too,
Show'd long since what our tongue could do;
Nor Lucan we, nor Horace spared;
Only Lucretius was too hard.
Lucretius, like a fort, did stand
Untouch'd, till your victorious hand
Did from his head this garland bear,
Which now upon your own you wear:
A garland made of such new bays,
And sought in such untrodden ways,
As no man's temples e'er did crown,
Save this great author's, and your own!

FOOTNOTE

[1] 'Master Evelyn': the well-known author of 'Sylva,' translated the first book of Lucretius, 'De Rerum Natura.'

TO HIS WORTHY FRIEND SIR THOMAS HIGGONS,[1] UPON HIS TRANSLATION OF 'THE VENETIAN TRIUMPH.'

The winged lion's not so fierce in fight
As Liberi's hand presents him to our sight;
Nor would his pencil make him half so fierce,
Or roar so loud, as Businello's verse;
But your translation does all three excel,
The fight, the piece, and lofty Businel.
As their small galleys may not hold compare
With our tall ships, whose sails employ more air;
So does th'Italian to your genius vail,
Moved with a fuller and a nobler gale.
Thus, while your Muse spreads the Venetian story,
You make all Europe emulate her glory;
You make them blush weak Venice should defend
The cause of Heaven, while they for words contend;
Shed Christian blood, and pop'lous cities raze,
Because they're taught to use some different phrase.
If, list'ning to your charms, we could our jars
Compose, and on the Turk discharge these wars,
Our British arms the sacred tomb might wrest
From Pagan hands, and triumph o'er the East;
And then you might our own high deeds recite,
And with great Tasso celebrate the fight.

FOOTNOTE

[1] 'Sir T. Higgons': a knight of some note, who translated the 'Venetian Triumph,' an Italian poem by Businello, addressed to Liberi, the painter.

TO A LADY SINGING A SONG OF HIS COMPOSING

I
Chloris! yourself you so excel,
When you vouchsafe to breathe my thought,
That, like a spirit, with this spell
Of my own teaching, I am caught.

II
That eagle's fate[1] and mine are one,
Which, on the shaft that made him die,
Espied a feather of his own,
Wherewith he wont to soar so high.

III
Had Echo, with so sweet a grace,
Narcissus' loud complaints return'd,
Not for reflection of his face,
But of his voice, the boy had burn'd.

FOOTNOTE
[1] 'Eagle's fate': Byron copies this thought in his verses on Kirke White

TO THE MUTABLE FAIR

Here, Cælia! for thy sake I part
With all that grew so near my heart;
The passion that I had for thee,
The faith, the love, the constancy!
And, that I may successful prove,
Transform myself to what you love.

Fool that I was! so much to prize
Those simple virtues you despise;
Fool! that with such dull arrows strove,
Or hoped to reach a flying dove;
For you, that are in motion still,
Decline our force, and mock our skill;
Who, like Don Quixote, do advance
Against a windmill our vain lance.

Now will I wander through the air,
Mount, make a stoop at every fair;

And, with a fancy unconfined
(As lawless as the sea or wind),
Pursue you wheresoe'er you fly,
And with your various thoughts comply.

The formal stars do travel so,
As we their names and courses know;
And he that on their changes looks,
Would think them govern'd by our books;
But never were the clouds reduced
To any art; the motions used
By those free vapours are so light,
So frequent, that the conquer'd sight
Despairs to find the rules that guide
Those gilded shadows as they slide;
And therefore of the spacious air,
Jove's royal consort had the care;
And by that power did once escape,
Declining bold Ixion's rape;
She with her own resemblance graced
A shining cloud, which he embraced.

Such was that image, so it smiled
With seeming kindness which beguiled
Your Thyrsis lately, when he thought
He had his fleeting Cælia caught.
'Twas shaped like her, but, for the fair,
He fill'd his arms with yielding air.

A fate for which he grieves the less,
Because the gods had like success;
For in their story one, we see,
Pursues a nymph, and takes a tree;
A second, with a lover's haste,
Soon overtakes whom he had chased,
But she that did a virgin seem,
Possess'd, appears a wand'ring stream;
For his supposed love, a third
Lays greedy hold upon a bird,
And stands amazed to find his dear
A wild inhabitant of the air.

To these old tales such nymphs as you
Give credit, and still make them new;
The am'rous now like wonders find
In the swift changes of your mind.

But, Cælia, if you apprehend

The Muse of your incensèd friend,
Nor would that he record your blame,
And make it live, repeat the same;
Again deceive him, and again,
And then he swears he'll not complain;
For still to be deluded so,
Is all the pleasure lovers know;
Who, like good falc'ners, take delight,
Not in the quarry, but the flight.

TO A LADY, FROM WHOM HE RECEIVED A SILVER PEN

I

Madam! intending to have tried
The silver favour which you gave,
In ink the shining point I dyed,
And drench'd it in the sable wave;
When, grieved to be so foully stain'd,
On you it thus to me complain'd.

II

'Suppose you had deserved to take
From her fair hand so fair a boon,
Yet how deservèd I to make
So ill a change, who ever won
Immortal praise for what I wrote,
Instructed by her noble thought?

III

'I, that expressed her commands
To mighty lords, and princely dames,
Always most welcome to their hands,
Proud that I would record their names,
Must now be taught an humble style,
Some meaner beauty to beguile!'

IV

So I, the wronged pen to please,
Make it my humble thanks express
Unto your ladyship, in these:
And now 'tis forcèd to confess
That your great self did ne'er indite,
Nor that, to one more noble, write.

TO CHLORIS

Chloris! since first our calm of peace
Was frighted hence, this good we find,
Your favours with your fears increase,
And growing mischiefs make you kind.

So the fair tree, which still preserves
Her fruit and state while no wind blows,
In storms from that uprightness swerves,
And the glad earth about her strows
With treasure, from her yielding boughs.

TO A LADY IN RETIREMENT

I
Sees not my love how time resumes
The glory which he lent these flowers?
Though none should taste of their perfumes,
Yet must they live but some few hours:
Time what we forbear devours!

II
Had Helen, or the Egyptian Queen,[1]
Been ne'er so thrifty of their graces,
Those beauties must at length have been
The spoil of age, which finds out faces
In the most retirèd places.

III
Should some malignant planet bring
A barren drought, or ceaseless shower,
Upon the autumn or the spring,
And spare us neither fruit nor flower;
Winter would not stay an hour.

IV
Could the resolve of love's neglect
Preserve you from the violation
Of coming years, then more respect
Were due to so divine a fashion,
Nor would I indulge my passion.

FOOTNOTE
[1] 'Egyptian Queen': Cleopatra.

TO MR GEORGE SANDYS,[1] ON HIS TRANSLATION OF SOME PARTS OF THE BIBLE

I

How bold a work attempts that pen,
Which would enrich our vulgar tongue
With the high raptures of those men
Who, here, with the same spirit sung
Wherewith they now assist the choir
Of angels, who their songs admire!

II

Whatever those inspirèd souls
Were urgèd to express, did shake
The aged deep and both the poles;
Their num'rous thunder could awake
Dull earth, which does with Heaven consent
To all they wrote, and all they meant.

III

Say, sacred bard! what could bestow
Courage on thee to soar so high?
Tell me, brave friend! what help'd thee so
To shake off all mortality?
To light this torch, thou hast climb'd higher
Than he who stole celestial fire.[2]

FOOTNOTES
[1] 'Sandys,' besides his 'Ovid,' which Pope read and relished in his boyhood, versified some of the poetical parts of the Bible.
[2] 'Celestial fire': Prometheus.

TO THE KING, UPON HIS MAJESTY'S HAPPY RETURN

The rising sun complies with our weak sight,
First gilds the clouds, then shows his globe of light
At such a distance from our eyes, as though
He knew what harm his hasty beams would do.

But your full majesty at once breaks forth
In the meridian of your reign. Your worth,
Your youth, and all the splendour of your state,
(Wrapp'd up, till now, in clouds of adverse fate!)
With such a flood of light invade our eyes,
And our spread hearts with so great joy surprise,

That if your grace incline that we should live,
You must not, sir! too hastily forgive.
Our guilt preserves us from th'excess of joy,
Which scatters spirits, and would life destroy.
All are obnoxious! and this faulty land,
Like fainting Esther, does before you stand,
Watching your sceptre. The revolted sea
Trembles to think she did your foes obey.

Great Britain, like blind Polypheme, of late,
In a wild rage, became the scorn and hate
Of her proud neighbours, who began to think
She, with the weight of her own force, would sink.
But you are come, and all their hopes are vain;
This giant isle has got her eye again.
Now she might spare the ocean, and oppose
Your conduct to the fiercest of her foes.
Naked, the Graces guarded you from all
Dangers abroad; and now your thunder shall.
Princes that saw you, diff'rent passions prove,
For now they dread the object of their love;
Nor without envy can behold his height,
Whose conversation was their late delight.
So Semele, contented with the rape
Of Jove disguisèd in a mortal shape,
When she beheld his hands with lightning fill'd,
And his bright rays, was with amazement kill'd.

And though it be our sorrow, and our crime,
To have accepted life so long a time
Without you here, yet does this absence gain
No small advantage to your present reign;
For, having view'd the persons and the things,
The councils, state, and strength of Europe's kings,
You know your work; ambition to restrain,
And set them bounds, as Heaven does to the main.
We have you now with ruling wisdom fraught,
Not such as books, but such as practice, taught.
So the lost sun, while least by us enjoy'd,
Is the whole night for our concern employ'd;
He ripens spices, fruits, and precious gums,
Which from remotest regions hither comes.

This seat of yours (from th'other world removed)
Had Archimedes known, he might have proved
His engine's force, fix'd here; your power and skill
Make the world's motion wait upon your will.

Much suffring monarch! the first English born
That has the crown of these three nations worn!
How has your patience, with the barb'rous rage
Of your own soil, contended half an age?
Till (your tried virtue, and your sacred word,
At last preventing your unwilling sword)
Armies and fleets which kept you out so long,
Own'd their great sov'reign, and redress'd his wrong;
When straight the people, by no force compell'd,
Nor longer from their inclination held,
Break forth at once, like powder set on fire,
And, with a noble rage, their king require.
So th'injured sea, which from her wonted course,
To gain some acres, avarice did force,
If the new banks, neglected once, decay,
No longer will from her old channel stay;
Raging, the late got land she overflows,
And all that's built upon't to ruin goes.

Offenders now, the chiefest, do begin
To strive for grace, and expiate their sin.
All winds blow fair, that did the world embroil;
Your vipers treacle yield, and scorpions oil.

If then such praise the Macedonian[1] got,
For having rudely cut the Gordian knot,
What glory's due to him that could divide
Such ravell'd interests; has the knot untied,
And without stroke so smooth a passage made,
Where craft and malice such impeachments laid?

But while we praise you, you ascribe it all
To His high hand, which threw the untouch'd wall
Of self-demolish'd Jericho so low;
His angel 'twas that did before you go,
Tamed savage hearts, and made affections yield,
Like ears of corn when wind salutes the field.

Thus, patience-crown'd, like Job's, your trouble ends,
Having your foes to pardon, and your friends;
For, though your courage were so firm a rock,
What private virtue could endure the shock?
Like your Great Master, you the storm withstood,
And pitied those who love with frailty show'd.

Rude Indians, tort'ring all the royal race,
Him with the throne and dear-bought sceptre grace
That suffers best. What region could be found,

Where your heroic head had not been crown'd?

The next experience of your mighty mind
Is, how you combat Fortune, now she's kind.
And this way, too, you are victorious found;
She flatters with the same success she frown'd.
While to yourself severe, to others kind,
With pow'r unbounded, and a will confined,
Of this vast empire you possess the care,
The softer parts fall to the people's share.
Safety, and equal government, are things
Which subjects make as happy as their kings.

Faith, Law, and Piety, (that banished train!)
Justice and Truth, with you return again.
The city's trade, and country's easy life,
Once more shall flourish without fraud or strife.
Your reign no less assures the ploughman's peace,
Than the warm sun advances his increase;
And does the shepherds as securely keep
From all their fears, as they preserve their sheep.

But, above all, the Muse-inspirèd train
Triumph, and raise their drooping heads again!
Kind Heaven at once has, in your person, sent
Their sacred judge, their guard, and argument.

Nec magis expressi vultus per ahenea signa,
Quam per vatis opus mores, animique, virorum
Clarorum apparent....
HOR.

FOOTNOTE
[1] *'Macedonian': Alexander.*

TO A LADY, FROM WHOM HE RECEIVED THE COPY OF THE POEM ENTITLED 'OF A TREE CUT IN PAPER,'
WHICH FOR MANY YEARS HAD BEEN LOST

Nothing lies hid from radiant eyes;
All they subdue become their spies.
Secrets, as choicest jewels, are
Presented to oblige the fair;
No wonder, then, that a lost thought
Should there be found, where souls are caught.

The picture of fair Venus (that
For which men say the goddess sat)
Was lost, till Lely from your book
Again that glorious image took.

If Virtue's self were lost, we might
From your fair mind new copies write.
All things but one you can restore;
The heart you get returns no more.

TO THE QUEEN, UPON HER MAJESTY'S BIRTHDAY, AFTER HER HAPPY RECOVERY FROM A DANGEROUS
SICKNESS [1]

Farewell the year! which threaten'd so
The fairest light the world can show.
Welcome the new! whose every day,
Restoring what was snatch'd away
By pining sickness from the fair,
That matchless beauty does repair
So fast, that the approaching spring
(Which does to flow'ry meadows bring
What the rude winter from them tore)
Shall give her all she had before.

But we recover not so fast
The sense of such a danger past;
We that esteem'd you sent from heaven,
A pattern to this island given,
To show us what the bless'd do there,
And what alive they practised here,
When that which we immortal thought,
We saw so near destruction brought,
Felt all which you did then endure,
And tremble yet, as not secure.
So though the sun victorious be,
And from a dark eclipse set free,
The influence, which we fondly fear,
Afflicts our thoughts the following year.

But that which may relieve our care
Is, that you have a help so near
For all the evil you can prove,
The kindness of your royal love;
He that was never known to mourn,
So many kingdoms from him torn,
His tears reserved for you, more dear,

More prized, than all those kingdoms were!
For when no healing art prevail'd,
When cordials and elixirs fail'd,
On your pale cheek he dropp'd the shower,
Revived you like a dying flower.

FOOTNOTE

[1] 'Dangerous sickness': the Queen of Charles II. These verses belong to the year 1663.

TO MR KILLIGREW,[1] UPON HIS ALTERING HIS PLAY, 'PANDORA,' FROM A TRAGEDY INTO A COMEDY, BECAUSE NOT APPROVED ON THE STAGE

Sir, you should rather teach our age the way
Of judging well, than thus have changed your play;
You had obliged us by employing wit,
Not to reform Pandora, but the pit;
For as the nightingale, without the throng
Of other birds, alone attends her song,
While the loud daw, his throat displaying, draws
The whole assemblage of his fellow-daws;
So must the writer, whose productions should
Take with the vulgar, be of vulgar mould;
Whilst nobler fancies make a flight too high
For common view, and lessen as they fly.

FOOTNOTE

[1] 'Mr. Killigrew': a gentleman usher to Charles II., and one of the playwrights of the period.

TO A PERSON OF HONOUR, UPON HIS INCOMPARABLE, INCOMPREHENSIBLE POEM, ENTITLED, 'THE BRITISH PRINCES.'[1]

Sir! you've obliged the British nation more
Than all their bards could ever do before,
And, at your own charge, monuments as hard
As brass or marble to your fame have rear'd;
For, as all warlike nations take delight
To hear how their brave ancestors could fight,
You have advanced to wonder their renown,
And no less virtuously improved your own;
That 'twill be doubtful whether you do write,
Or they have acted, at a nobler height.
You of your ancient princes, have retrieved
More than the ages knew in which they lived;
Explain'd their customs and their rights anew,

Better than all their Druids ever knew;
Unriddled those dark oracles as well
As those that made them could themselves foretell.
For as the Britons long have hoped, in vain,
Arthur would come to govern them again,
You have fulfill'd that prophecy alone,
And in your poem placed him on his throne.
Such magic power has your prodigious pen
To raise the dead, and give new life to men,
Make rival princes meet in arms and love,
Whom distant ages did so far remove;
For as eternity has neither past
Nor future, authors say, nor first nor last,
But is all instant, your eternal Muse
All ages can to any one reduce.
Then why should you, whose miracles of art
Can life at pleasure to the dead impart,
Trouble in vain your better-busied head,
T'observe what times they lived in, or were dead?
For since you have such arbitrary power,
It were defect in judgment to go lower,
Or stoop to things so pitifully lewd,
As use to take the vulgar latitude;
For no man's fit to read what you have writ,
That holds not some proportion with your wit;
As light can no way but by light appear,
He must bring sense that understands it here.

FOOTNOTE

[1] 'The British Princes': an heroic poem, by the Hon. Edward Howard, was universally laughed at. See our edition of 'Butler.'

TO A FRIEND OF THE AUTHOR, A PERSON OF HONOUR, WHO LATELY WRIT A RELIGIOUS BOOK, ENTITLED, 'HISTORICAL APPLICATIONS, AND OCCASIONAL MEDITATIONS, UPON SEVERAL SUBJECTS.'[1]

Bold is the man that dares engage
For piety in such an age!
Who can presume to find a guard
From scorn, when Heaven's so little spared?
Divines are pardon'd; they defend
Altars on which their lives depend;
But the profane impatient are,
When nobler pens make this their care;
For why should these let in a beam
Of divine light to trouble them,

And call in doubt their pleasing thought,
That none believes what we are taught?
High birth and fortune warrant give
That such men write what they believe;
And, feeling first what they indite,
New credit give to ancient light.
Amongst these few, our author brings
His well-known pedigree from kings.[2]
This book, the image of his mind,
Will make his name not hard to find;
I wish the throng of great and good
Made it less eas'ly understood!

FOOTNOTES

[1] 'Several subjects': supposed to be Lord Berkeley. It contained testimonies of celebrated men to the value of religion.
[2] 'Pedigree from kings': the Earl of Berkeley was descended from the royal house of Denmark.

TO THE DUCHESS OF ORLEANS, WHEN SHE WAS TAKING LEAVE OF THE COURT AT DOVER [1]

That sun of beauty did among us rise;
England first saw the light of your fair eyes;
In English, too, your early wit was shown;
Favour that language, which was then your own,
When, though a child, through guards you made your way;
What fleet or army could an angel stay?
Thrice happy Britain! if she could retain
Whom she first bred within her ambient main.
Our late burnt London, in apparel new,
Shook off her ashes to have treated you;
But we must see our glory snatch'd away,
And with warm tears increase the guilty sea;
No wind can favour us; howe'er it blows,
We must be wreck'd, and our dear treasure lose!
Sighs will not let us half our sorrows tell,—
Fair, lovely, great, and best of nymphs, farewell!

FOOTNOTE

[1] 'Court at Dover': the Duchess of Orleans, the youngest daughter of Charles I., came to England on the 14th May 1670, on a political mission.

TO CHLORIS

Chloris! what's eminent, we know

Must for some cause be valued so;
Things without use, though they be good,
Are not by us so understood.
The early rose, made to display
Her blushes to the youthful May,
Doth yield her sweets, since he is fair,
And courts her with a gentle air.
Our stars do show their excellence
Not by their light, but influence;
When brighter comets, since still known
Fatal to all, are liked by none.
So your admirèd beauty still
Is, by effects, made good or ill.

TO THE KING

Great Sir! disdain not in this piece to stand,
Supreme commander both of sea and land.
Those which inhabit the celestial bower,
Painters express with emblems of their power;
His club Alcides, Phoebus has his bow,
Jove has his thunder, and your navy you.

But your great providence no colours here
Can represent, nor pencil draw that care,
Which keeps you waking to secure our peace,
The nation's glory, and our trade's increase;
You, for these ends, whole days in council sit,
And the diversions of your youth forget.

Small were the worth of valour and of force,
If your high wisdom governed not their course;
You as the soul, as the first mover you,
Vigour and life on every part bestow;
How to build ships, and dreadful ordnance cast,
Instruct the artists, and reward their haste.

So Jove himself, when Typhon heaven does brave,
Descends to visit Vulcan's smoky cave,
Teaching the brawny Cyclops how to frame
His thunder, mix'd with terror, wrath, and flame.
Had the old Greeks discover'd your abode,
Crete had not been the cradle of their god;
On that small island they had looked with scorn,
And in Great Britain thought the Thunderer born.

TO THE DUCHESS, WHEN HE PRESENTED THIS BOOK TO HER ROYAL HIGHNESS

Madam! I here present you with the rage,
And with the beauties of a former age;
Wishing you may with as great pleasure view
This, as we take in gazing upon you.
Thus we writ then: your brighter eyes inspire
A nobler flame, and raise our genius higher.
While we your wit and early knowledge fear,
To our productions we become severe;
Your matchless beauty gives our fancy wing,
Your judgment makes us careful how we sing.
Lines not composed, as heretofore, in haste,
Polish'd like marble, shall like marble last,
And make you through as many ages shine,
As Tasso has the heroes of your line.

Though other names our wary writers use,
You are the subject of the British Muse;
Dilating mischief to yourself unknown,
Men write, and die of wounds they dare not own.
So the bright sun burns all our grass away,
While it means nothing but to give us day.

TO MR CREECH, ON HIS TRANSLATION OF 'LUCRETIUS.'[1]

What all men wish'd, though few could hope to see,
We are now bless'd with, and obliged by thee.
Thou, from the ancient, learned Latin store,
Giv'st us one author, and we hope for more.
May they enjoy thy thoughts!—Let not the stage
The idlest moment of thy hours engage;
Each year that place some wondrous monster breeds,
And the wits' garden is o'errun with weeds.
There, Farce is Comedy; bombast called strong;
Soft words, with nothing in them, make a song.
'Tis hard to say they steal them now-a-days;
For sure the ancients never wrote such plays.
These scribbling insects have what they deserve,
Not plenty, nor the glory for to starve.
That Spenser knew, that Tasso felt before;
And death found surly Ben exceeding poor.
Heaven turn the omen from their image here!
May he with joy the well-placed laurel wear!

Great Virgil's happier fortune may he find,
And be our Cæsar, like Augustus, kind!

But let not this disturb thy tuneful head;
Thou writ'st for thy delight, and not for bread;
Thou art not cursed to write thy verse with care;
But art above what other poets fear.
What may we not expect from such a hand,
That has, with books, himself at free command?
Thou know'st in youth, what age has sought in vain;
And bring'st forth sons without a mother's pain.
So easy is thy sense, thy verse so sweet,
Thy words so proper, and thy phrase so fit,
We read, and read again; and still admire
Whence came this youth, and whence this wondrous fire!

Pardon this rapture, sir! but who can be
Cold, and unmoved, yet have his thoughts on thee?
Thy goodness may my several faults forgive,
And by your help these wretched lines may live.
But if, when view'd by your severer sight,
They seem unworthy to behold the light,
Let them with speed in deserv'd flames be thrown!
They'll send no sighs, nor murmur out a groan;
But, dying silently, your justice own.

FOOTNOTE
[1] 'Lucretius': this piece is not contained in Anderson, or the edition of 1693.

SONGS

STAY, PHOEBUS!

I
Stay, Phoebus! stay;
The world to which you fly so fast,
Conveying day
From us to them, can pay your haste
With no such object, nor salute your rise,
With no such wonder as De Mornay's eyes.

II
Well does this prove
The error of those antique books,
Which made you move
About the world; her charming looks

Would fix your beams, and make it ever day,
Did not the rolling earth snatch her away.

PEACE, BABBLING MUSE!

Peace, babbling Muse!
I dare not sing what you indite;
Her eyes refuse
To read the passion which they write.
She strikes my lute, but, if it sound,
Threatens to hurl it on the ground;
And I no less her anger dread,
Than the poor wretch that feigns him dead,
While some fierce lion does embrace
His breathless corpse, and lick his face;
Wrapp'd up in silent fear he lies,
Torn all in pieces if he cries.

CHLORIS! FAREWELL

I
Chloris! farewell. I now must go;
For if with thee I longer stay,
Thy eyes prevail upon me so,
I shall prove blind, and lose my way.

II
Fame of thy beauty, and thy youth,
Among the rest, me hither brought;
Finding this fame fall short of truth,
Made me stay longer than I thought.

III
For I'm engaged by word and oath,
A servant to another's will;
Yet, for thy love, I'd forfeit both,
Could I be sure to keep it still.

IV
But what assurance can I take,
When thou, foreknowing this abuse,
For some more worthy lover's sake,
Mayst leave me with so just excuse?

V

For thou mayst say, 'twas not thy fault
That thou didst thus inconstant prove;
Being by my example taught
To break thy oath, to mend thy love.

VI

No, Chloris! no: I will return,
And raise thy story to that height,
That strangers shall at distance burn,
And she distrust me reprobate.

VII

Then shall my love this doubt displace,
And gain such trust, that I may come
And banquet sometimes on thy face,
But make my constant meals at home.

TO FLAVIA

I

'Tis not your beauty can engage
My wary heart;
The sun, in all his pride and rage,
Has not that art;
And yet he shines as bright as you,
If brightness could our souls subdue.

II

'Tis not the pretty things you say,
Nor those you write,
Which can make Thyrsis' heart your prey:
For that delight,
The graces of a well-taught mind,
In some of our own sex we find.

III

No, Flavia! 'tis your love I fear;
Love's surest darts,
Those which so seldom fail him, are
Headed with hearts;
Their very shadows make us yield;
Dissemble well, and win the field.

BEHOLD THE BRAND OF BEAUTY TOSS'D!

I

Behold the brand of beauty toss'd!
See how the motion does dilate the flame!
Delighted Love his spoils does boast,
And triumph in this game.
Fire, to no place confined,
Is both our wonder and our fear;
Moving the mind,
As lightning hurlèd through the air.

II

High heaven the glory does increase
Of all her shining lamps, this artful way;
The sun in figures, such as these,
Joys with the moon to play;
To the sweet strains they advance,
Which do result from their own spheres,
As this nymph's dance
Moves with the numbers which she hears.

WHILE I LISTEN TO THY VOICE

I

While I listen to thy voice,
Chloris! I feel my life decay;
That powerful noise
Calls my fleeting soul away.
Oh! suppress that magic sound,
Which destroys without a wound.

II

Peace, Chloris! peace! or singing die,
That together you and I
To heaven may go;
For all we know
Of what the blessed do above,
Is, that they sing, and that they love.

GO, LOVELY ROSE!

I

Go, lovely Rose!

Tell her that wastes her time and me,
That now she knows,
When I resemble her to thee,
How sweet and fair she seems to be.

II
Tell her that's young,
And shuns to have her graces spied,
That hadst thou sprung
In deserts, where no men abide,
Thou must have uncommended died.

III
Small is the worth
Of beauty from the light retired;
Bid her come forth,
Suffer herself to be desired,
And not blush so to be admired.

IV
Then die! that she
The common fate of all things rare
May read in thee;
How small a part of time they share
That are so wondrous sweet and fair!

This happy day two lights are seen,
A glorious saint, a matchless queen;[1]
Both named alike, both crown'd appear,
The saint above, th'Infanta here.
May all those years which Catherine
The martyr did for heaven resign,
Be added to the line
Of your bless'd life among us here!
For all the pains that she did feel,
And all the torments of her wheel,
May you as many pleasures share!
May heaven itself content
With Catherine the Saint!
Without appearing old,
An hundred times may you,
With eyes as bright as now,
This welcome day behold!

SONG

I

Say, lovely dream! where couldst thou find
Shades to counterfeit that face?
Colours of this glorious kind
Come not from any mortal place.

II

In heaven itself thou sure wert dress'd
With that angel-like disguise:
Thus deluded am I bless'd,
And see my joy with closèd eyes.

III

But, ah! this image is too kind
To be other than a dream;
Cruel Saccharissa's mind
Never put on that sweet extreme!

IV

Fair dream! if thou intend'st me grace,
Change that heavenly face of thine;
Paint despised love in thy face,
And make it to appear like mine.

V

Pale, wan, and meagre let it look,
With a pity-moving shape,
Such as wander by the brook
Of Lethe, or from graves escape.

VI

Then to that matchless nymph appear,
In whose shape thou shinest so;
Softly in her sleeping ear,
With humble words, express my woe.

VII

Perhaps from greatness, state, and pride,
Thus surprisèd she may fall;
Sleep does disproportion hide,
And, death resembling, equals all.

PROLOGUE FOR THE LADY-ACTORS. SPOKEN BEFORE KING CHARLES II

Amaze us not with that majestic frown,
But lay aside the greatness of your crown!
And for that look which does your people awe,
When in your throne and robes you give them law,
Lay it by here, and give a gentler smile,
Such as we see great Jove's in picture, while
He listens to Apollo's charming lyre,
Or judges of the songs he does inspire.
Comedians on the stage show all their skill,
And after do as Love and Fortune will.
We are less careful, hid in this disguise;
In our own clothes more serious and more wise.
Modest at home, upon the stage more bold,
We seem warm lovers, though our breasts be cold;
A fault committed here deserves no scorn,
If we act well the parts to which we're born.

PROLOGUE TO THE 'MAID'S TRAGEDY' [1]

Scarce should we have the boldness to pretend
So long-renown'd a tragedy to mend,
Had not already some deserved your praise
With like attempt. Of all our elder plays
This and Philaster have the loudest fame;
Great are their faults, and glorious is their flame.
In both our English genius is express'd;   7
Lofty and bold, but negligently dress'd.

Above our neighbours our conceptions are;
But faultless writing is th'effect of care.
Our lines reform'd, and not composed in haste,
Polished like marble, would like marble last.[2]
But as the present, so the last age writ;
In both we find like negligence and wit.
Were we but less indulgent to our faults,
And patience had to cultivate our thoughts,
Our Muse would flourish, and a nobler rage
Would honour this than did the Grecian stage.

Thus says our author, not content to see
That others write as carelessly as he;
Though he pretends not to make things complete,
Yet, to please you, he'd have the poets sweat.

In this old play, what's new we have express'd
In rhyming verse, distinguish'd from the rest;
That as the Rhone its hasty way does make
(Not mingling waters) through Geneva's lake,
So having here the different styles in view,
You may compare the former with the new.

If we less rudely shall the knot untie,
Soften the rigour of the tragedy,
And yet preserve each person's character,
Then to the other this you may prefer.
'Tis left to you: the boxes and the pit,
Are sov'reign judges of this sort of wit.
In other things the knowing artist may
Judge better than the people; but a play,
(Made for delight, and for no other use)
If you approve it not, has no excuse.

FOOTNOTES
[1] 'Maid's Tragedy': Waller altered this tragedy without success.
[2] 'Marble last': these lines occur in a previous poem.

EPILOGUE TO THE 'MAID'S TRAGEDY.' SPOKEN BY THE KING

The fierce Melantius was content, you see,
The king should live; be not more fierce than he;
Too long indulgent to so rude a time,
When love was held so capital a crime,
That a crown'd head could no compassion find,
But died—because the killer had been kind!
Nor is't less strange, such mighty wits as those
Should use a style in tragedy like prose.
Well-sounding verse, where princes tread the stage,
Should speak their virtue, or describe their rage.
By the loud trumpet, which our courage aids,
We learn that sound, as well as sense, persuades;
And verses are the potent charms we use,
Heroic thoughts and virtue to infuse.

When next we act this tragedy again,

Unless you like the change, we shall be slain.
The innocent Aspasia's life or death,
Amintor's too, depends upon your breath.
Excess of love was heretofore the cause;
Now if we die, 'tis want of your applause.

Aspasia bleeding on the stage does lie,
To show you still 'tis the Maid's Tragedy.
The fierce Melantius was content, you see,
The king should live; be not more fierce than he;
Too long indulgent to so rude a time,
When love was held so capital a crime,
That a crown'd head could no compassion find,
But died—because the killer had been kind!
This better-natured poet had reprieved
Gentle Amintor too, had he believed
The fairer sex his pardon could approve,
Who to ambition sacrificed his love.
Aspasia he has spared; but for her wound
(Neglected love!) there could no salve be found.

When next we act this tragedy again,
Unless you like the change, I must be slain.
Excess of love was heretofore the cause;
Now if I die, 'tis want of your applause.

EPIGRAMS, EPITAPHS, AND FRAGMENTS

UNDER A LADY'S PICTURE

Such Helen was! and who can blame the boy[1]
That in so bright a flame consumed his Troy?
But had like virtue shined in that fair Greek,
The am'rous shepherd had not dared to seek
Or hope for pity; but with silent moan,
And better fate, had perished alone.

FOOTNOTE
[1] Paris.

OF A LADY WHO WRIT IN PRAISE OF MIRA

While she pretends to make the graces known
Of matchless Mira, she reveals her own;
And when she would another's praise indite,
Is by her glass instructed how to write.

TO ONE MARRIED TO AN OLD MAN

Since thou wouldst needs (bewitch'd with some ill charms!)
Be buried in those monumental arms,
All we can wish is, may that earth lie light
Upon thy tender limbs! and so good night.

AN EPIGRAM ON A PAINTED LADY WITH ILL TEETH

Were men so dull they could not see
That Lyce painted; should they flee,
Like simple birds, into a net
So grossly woven and ill set,
Her own teeth would undo the knot,
And let all go that she had got.
Those teeth fair Lyce must not show
If she would bite; her lovers, though
Like birds they stoop at seeming grapes,
Are disabused when first she gapes;
The rotten bones discover'd there,
Show 'tis a painted sepulchre.

EPIGRAM UPON THE GOLDEN MEDAL [1]

Our guard upon the royal side!
On the reverse our beauty's pride!
Here we discern the frown and smile,
The force and glory of our isle.
In the rich medal, both so like
Immortals stand, it seems antique;
Carved by some master, when the bold
Greeks made their Jove descend in gold,
And Danaë wond'ring at their shower,
Which, falling, storm'd her brazen tower.

Britannia there, the fort in vain
Had batter'd been with golden rain;
Thunder itself had fail'd to pass;
Virtue's a stronger guard than brass.

FOOTNOTE

[1] 'Golden Medal': it is said that a Miss Stewart, the favourite of the unprincipled king, is the original of the figure of Britannia on the medals to which the poet here alludes.

WRITTEN ON A CARD THAT HER MAJESTY TORE AT OMBRE

The cards you tear in value rise;
So do the wounded by your eyes.
Who to celestial things aspire,
Are by that passion raised the higher.

TO MR GRANVILLE (NOW LORD LANSDOWNE), ON HIS VERSES TO KING JAMES II

An early plant! which such a blossom bears,
And shows a genius so beyond his years;
A judgment! that could make so fair a choice;
So high a subject to employ his voice;
Still as it grows, how sweetly will he sing
The growing greatness of our matchless king!

LONG AND SHORT LIFE

Circles are praised, not that abound
In largeness, but th'exactly round:
So life we praise that does excel
Not in much time, but acting well.

TRANSLATED OUT OF SPANISH

Though we may seem importunate,
While your compassion we implore;
They whom you make too fortunate,
May with presumption vex you more.

TRANSLATED OUT OF FRENCH

Fade, flowers! fade, Nature will have it so;
'Tis but what we must in our autumn do!
And as your leaves lie quiet on the ground,
The loss alone by those that loved them found;
So in the grave shall we as quiet lie,
Miss'd by some few that loved our company;
But some so like to thorns and nettles live,
That none for them can, when they perish, grieve.

SOME VERSES OF AN IMPERFECT COPY, DESIGNED FOR A FRIEND, ON HIS TRANSLATION OF OVID'S 'FASTI.'

Rome's holy-days you tell, as if a guest
With the old Romans you were wont to feast.
Numa's religion, by themselves believed,
Excels the true, only in show received.
They made the nations round about them bow,
With their dictators taken from the plough;
Such power has justice, faith, and honesty!
The world was conquer'd by morality.
Seeming devotion does but gild a knave,
That's neither faithful, honest, just, nor brave;
But where religion does with virtue join,
It makes a hero like an angel shine.

ON THE STATUE OF KING CHARLES I., AT CHARING CROSS, IN THE YEAR 1674

That the First Charles does here in triumph ride,
See his son reign where he a martyr died,
And people pay that rev'rence as they pass,
(Which then he wanted!) to the sacred brass,
Is not the effect of gratitude alone,
To which we owe the statue and the stone;
But Heaven this lasting monument has wrought,
That mortals may eternally be taught
Rebellion, though successful, is but vain,
And kings so kill'd rise conquerors again.
This truth the royal image does proclaim,
Loud as the trumpet of surviving Fame.

PRIDE

Not the brave Macedonian youth[1] alone,
But base Caligula, when on the throne,
Boundless in power, would make himself a god,
As if the world depended on his nod.
The Syrian king[2] to beasts was headlong thrown,
Ere to himself he could be mortal known.
The meanest wretch, if Heaven should give him line,
Would never stop till he were thought divine.
All might within discern the serpent's pride,
If from ourselves nothing ourselves did hide.
Let the proud peacock his gay feathers spread,
And woo the female to his painted bed;
Let winds and seas together rage and swell—
This Nature teaches, and becomes them well.
'Pride was not made for men;'[3] a conscious sense
Of guilt, and folly, and their consequence,
Destroys the claim, and to beholders tells,
Here nothing but the shape of manhood dwells.

FOOTNOTES
[1] 'Macedonian youth': Alexander.
[2] 'Syrian king': Nebuchadnezzar.
[3] 'For men': Ecclus. x. 18.

EPITAPH ON SIR GEORGE SPEKE

Under this stone lies virtue, youth,
Unblemish'd probity, and truth,
Just unto all relations known,
A worthy patriot, pious son;
Whom neighb'ring towns so often sent
To give their sense in Parliament;
With lives and fortunes trusting one
Who so discreetly used his own.
Sober he was, wise, temperate,
Contented with an old estate,
Which no foul avarice did increase,
Nor wanton luxury make less.
While yet but young his father died,
And left him to a happy guide;
Not Lemuel's mother with more care
Did counsel or instruct her heir,
Or teach with more success her son

The vices of the time to shun.
An heiress she; while yet alive,
All that was hers to him did give;
And he just gratitude did show
To one that had obliged him so;
Nothing too much for her he thought,
By whom he was so bred and taught.
So (early made that path to tread,
Which did his youth to honour lead)
His short life did a pattern give
How neighbours, husbands, friends, should live.

The virtues of a private life
Exceed the glorious noise and strife
Of battles won; in those we find
The solid int'rest of mankind.

Approved by all, and loved so well,
Though young, like fruit that's ripe, he fell.

EPITAPH ON COLONEL CHARLES CAVENDISH [1]

Here lies Charles Ca'ndish; let the marble stone
That hides his ashes make his virtue known.
Beauty and valour did his short life grace,
The grief and glory of his noble race!
Early abroad he did the world survey,
As if he knew he had not long to stay;
Saw what great Alexander in the East,
And mighty Julius conquer'd in the West;
Then, with a mind as great as theirs, he came
To find at home occasion for his fame;
Where dark confusion did the nations hide,
And where the juster was the weaker side.
Two loyal brothers took their sov'reign's part,
Employ'd their wealth, their courage, and their art;
The elder[2] did whole regiments afford;
The younger brought his conduct and his sword.
Born to command, a leader he begun,
And on the rebels lasting honour won.
The horse, instructed by their general's worth,
Still made the king victorious in the north.
Where Ca'ndish fought, the Royalists prevail'd;
Neither his courage nor his judgment fail'd.
The current of his vict'ries found no stop,
Till Cromwell came, his party's chiefest prop.

Equal success had set these champions high,
And both resolved to conquer or to die.
Virtue with rage, fury with valour strove;
But that must fall which is decreed above!
Cromwell, with odds of number and of fate,
Removed this bulwark of the church and state;
Which the sad issue of the war declared,
And made his task, to ruin both, less hard.
So when the bank, neglected, is o'erthrown,
The boundless torrent does the country drown.
Thus fell the young, the lovely, and the brave;—
Strew bays and flowers on his honoured grave!

FOOTNOTES

[1] 'Charles Cavendish': younger son of the Earl of Devonshire, and brother of Lady Rich; slain in 1643 at Gainsborough, fighting on the king's side, in the twenty-third year of his age.
[2] 'The elder': afterwards Earl of Devonshire.

EPITAPH ON THE LADY SEDLEY [1]

Here lies the learned Savil's heir,
So early wise, and lasting fair,
That none, except her years they told,
Thought her a child, or thought her old.
All that her father knew or got,
His art, his wealth, fell to her lot;
And she so well improved that stock,
Both of his knowledge and his flock,
That wit and fortune, reconciled
In her, upon each other smiled.
While she to every well-taught mind
Was so propitiously inclined,
And gave such title to her store,
That none, but th'ignorant, were poor.
The Muses daily found supplies,
Both from her hands and from her eyes.
Her bounty did at once engage,
And matchless beauty warm their rage.
Such was this dame in calmer days,
Her nation's ornament and praise!
But when a storm disturb'd our rest,
The port and refuge of the oppress'd.
This made her fortune understood,
And look'd on as some public good.
So that (her person and her state,
Exempted from the common fate)

In all our civil fury she
Stood, like a sacred temple, free.
May here her monument stand so,
To credit this rude age! and show
To future times, that even we
Some patterns did of virtue see;
And one sublime example had
Of good, among so many bad.

FOOTNOTE

[1] 'Lady Sedley': daughter of Sir Henry Savil, provost of Eton, and who married Sir John Sedley.

EPITAPH, TO BE WRITTEN UNDER THE LATIN INSCRIPTION UPON THE TOMB OF THE ONLY SON OF THE LORD ANDOVER [1]

'Tis fit the English reader should be told,
In our own language, what this tomb does hold.
'Tis not a noble corpse alone does lie
Under this stone, but a whole family.
His parents' pious care, their name, their joy,
And all their hope, lies buried with this boy;
This lovely youth! for whom we all made moan,
That knew his worth, as he had been our own.

Had there been space and years enough allow'd,
His courage, wit, and breeding to have show'd,
We had not found, in all the num'rous roll
Of his famed ancestors, a greater soul;
His early virtues to that ancient stock
Gave as much honour, as from thence he took.

Like buds appearing ere the frosts are past,
To become man he made such fatal haste,
And to perfection labour'd so to climb,
Preventing slow experience and time,
That 'tis no wonder Death our hopes beguiled;
He's seldom old that will not be a child.

FOOTNOTE

[1] 'Lord Andover': the eldest son of the Earl of Berkshire.

EPITAPH UNFINISHED

Great soul! for whom Death will no longer stay,

But sends in haste to snatch our bliss away.
O cruel Death! to those you take more kind,
Than to the wretched mortals left behind!
Here beauty, youth, and noble virtue shined,
Free from the clouds of pride that shade the mind.
Inspirèd verse may on this marble live,
But can no honour to thy ashes give—

DIVINE POEMS [1]

OF DIVINE LOVE. A POEM IN SIX CANTOS

Floriferis ut apes in saltibus omnia libant,
Sic nos Scripturæ depascimur aurea dicta;
Aurea! perpetua semper dignissima vita!
Nam divinus amor cum coepit vociferari,
Diffugiunt animi terrores....
Lucretius, lib. iii.

Exul eram, requiesque mihi, non fama, petita est,
Mens intenta suis ne foret usque malis:
Namque ubi mota calent sacra mea pectora Musa,
Altior humano spiritua ille malo est.
OVID. De Trist. lib. iv. el. I.

ARGUMENTS

I.
Asserting the authority of the Scripture, in which this love is revealed.—

II.
The preference and love of God to man in the creation.—

III.
The same love more amply declared in our redemption.—

IV.
How necessary this love is to reform mankind, and how excellent in itself.—

V.
Showing how happy the world would be, if this love were universally
embraced.—

VI.
Of preserving this love in our memory, and how useful the contemplation thereof is.

FOOTNOTE

[1] These were Waller's latest poems, composed when he was eighty-two.

CANTO I

The Grecian Muse has all their gods survived,
Nor Jove at us, nor Phoebus is arrived;
Frail deities! which first the poets made,
And then invoked, to give their fancies aid.
Yet if they still divert us with their rage,
What may be hoped for in a better age,
When not from Helicon's imagined spring,
But Sacred Writ, we borrow what we sing?
This with the fabric of the world begun,
Elder than light, and shall outlast the sun.
Before this oracle, like Dagon, all
The false pretenders, Delphos, Ammon, fall;
Long since despised and silent, they afford
Honour and triumph to th'Eternal Word.

As late philosophy[1] our globe has graced,
And rolling earth among the planets placed,
So has this book entitled us to heaven,
And rules to guide us to that mansion given;
Tells the conditions how our peace was made,
And is our pledge for the great Author's aid.
His power in Nature's ample book we find,
But the less volume does express his mind.

This light unknown, bold Epicurus taught
That his bless'd gods vouchsafe us not a thought,
But unconcern'd let all below them slide,
As fortune does, or human wisdom, guide.
Religion thus removed, the sacred yoke,
And band of all society, is broke.
What use of oaths, of promise, or of test,
Where men regard no God but interest?
What endless war would jealous nations tear,
If none above did witness what they swear?
Sad fate of unbelievers, and yet just,
Among themselves to find so little trust!
Were Scripture silent, Nature would proclaim,
Without a God, our falsehood and our shame.
To know our thoughts the object of his eyes,
Is the first step t'wards being good or wise;

For though with judgment we on things reflect,
Our will determines, not our intellect.
Slaves to their passion, reason men employ
Only to compass what they would enjoy.
His fear to guard us from ourselves we need,
And Sacred Writ our reason does exceed;
For though heaven shows the glory of the Lord,
Yet something shines more glorious in His Word;
His mercy this (which all His work excels!)
His tender kindness and compassion tells;
While we, inform'd by that celestial Book,
Into the bowels of our Maker look.
Love there reveal'd (which never shall have end,
Nor had beginning) shall our song commend;
Describe itself, and warm us with that flame
Which first from heaven, to make us happy, came.

FOOTNOTE
[1] 'Late philosophy': that of Copernicus.

CANTO II

The fear of hell, or aiming to be bless'd,
Savours too much of private interest.
This moved not Moses, nor the zealous Paul,
Who for their friends abandon'd soul and all;[1]
A greater yet from heaven to hell descends,
To save, and make his enemies his friends.
What line of praise can fathom such a love,
Which reach'd the lowest bottom from above?
The royal prophet,[2] that extended grace
From heaven to earth, measured but half that space.
The law was regnant, and confined his thought;
Hell was not conquer'd when that poet wrote;
Heaven was scarce heard of until He came down,
To make the region where love triumphs known.

That early love of creatures yet unmade,
To frame the world the Almighty did persuade;
For love it was that first created light,
Moved on the waters, chased away the night
From the rude Chaos, and bestow'd new grace
On things disposed of to their proper place;
Some to rest here, and some to shine above;
Earth, sea, and heaven, were all th'effects of love.
And love would be return'd; but there was none

That to themselves or others yet were known;
The world a palace was without a guest,
Till one appears that must excel the rest;
One! like the Author, whose capacious mind
Might, by the glorious work, the Maker find;
Might measure heaven, and give each star a name;
With art and courage the rough ocean tame;
Over the globe with swelling sails might go,
And that 'tis round by his experience know;
Make strongest beasts obedient to his will,
And serve his use the fertile earth to till.

When, by His Word, God had accomplish'd all,
Man to create He did a council call;
Employed His hand, to give the dust He took
A graceful figure, and majestic look;
With His own breath convey'd into his breast
Life, and a soul fit to command the rest;
Worthy alone to celebrate His name
For such a gift, and tell from whence it came.
Birds sing His praises in a wilder note,
But not with lasting numbers and with thought,
Man's great prerogative! but above all
His grace abounds in His new fav'rite's fall.

If He create, it is a world He makes;
If He be angry, the creation shakes;
From His just wrath our guilty parents fled;
He cursed the earth, but bruised the serpent's head.
Amidst the storm His bounty did exceed,
In the rich promise of the Virgin's seed;
Though justice death, as satisfaction, craves,
Love finds a way to pluck us from our graves.

FOOTNOTES
[1] 'Abandoned soul and all': Exodus xxxii. 32. Ep. to the Romans ix. 3.
[2]: 'Royal prophet': David.

CANTO III

Not willing terror should His image move;
He gives a pattern of eternal love;
His Son descends to treat a peace with those
Which were, and must have ever been, His foes.
Poor He became, and left His glorious seat
To make us humble, and to make us great;

His business here was happiness to give
To those whose malice could not let Him live.

Legions of angels, which He might have used,
(For us resolved to perish) He refused;
While they stood ready to prevent His loss,
Love took Him up, and nail'd Him to the cross.

Immortal love! which in His bowels reign'd,
That we might be by such great love constrain'd
To make return of love. Upon this pole
Our duty does, and our religion, roll.
To love is to believe, to hope, to know;
'Tis an essay, a taste of heaven below!

He to proud potentates would not be known;
Of those that loved Him He was hid from none.
Till love appear we live in anxious doubt;
But smoke will vanish when the flame breaks out;
This is the fire that would consume our dross,
Refine, and make us richer by the loss.

Could we forbear dispute, and practise love,
We should agree as angels do above.
Where love presides, not vice alone does find
No entrance there, but virtues stay behind;
Both faith, and hope, and all the meaner train
Of mortal virtues, at the door remain.
Love only enters as a native there,
For, born in heaven, it does but sojourn here.

He that alone would wise and mighty be,
Commands that others love as well as He.
Love as He loved!—How can we soar so high?—
He can add wings, when He commands to fly.
Nor should we be with this command dismay'd;
He that examples gives, will give His aid;
For He took flesh, that where His precepts fail,
His practice as a pattern may prevail.
His love, at once, and dread, instruct our thought;
As man He suffer'd, and as God He taught.
Will for the deed He takes; we may with ease
Obedient be, for if we love we please.
Weak though we are, to love is no hard task,
And love for love is all that Heaven does ask.
Love! that would all men just and temp'rate make,
Kind to themselves, and others, for His sake.

'Tis with our minds as with a fertile ground,
Wanting this love they must with weeds abound,
(Unruly passions), whose effects are worse
Than thorns and thistles springing from the curse.

CANTO IV

To glory man, or misery, is born,
Of his proud foe the envy, or the scorn;
Wretched he is, or happy, in extreme;
Base in himself, but great in Heaven's esteem;
With love, of all created things the best;
Without it, more pernicious than the rest;
For greedy wolves unguarded sheep devour
But while their hunger lasts, and then give o'er;
Man's boundless avarice his wants exceeds,
And on his neighbours round about him feeds.

His pride and vain ambition are so vast,
That, deluge-like, they lay whole nations waste.
Debauches and excess (though with less noise)
As great a portion of mankind destroys.
The beasts and monsters Hercules oppress'd,
Might in that age some provinces infest;
These more destructive monsters are the bane
Of every age, and in all nations reign;
But soon would vanish, if the world were bless'd
With sacred love, by which they are repress'd.

Impendent death, and guilt that threatens hell,
Are dreadful guests, which here with mortals dwell;
And a vex'd conscience, mingling with their joy
Thoughts of despair, does their whole life annoy;
But love appearing, all those terrors fly;
We live contented, and contented die.
They in whose breast this sacred love has place,
Death, as a passage to their joy, embrace.
Clouds and thick vapours, which obscure the day,
The sun's victorious beams may chase away;
Those which our life corrupt and darken, love
(The nobler star!) must from the soul remove.
Spots are observed in that which bounds the year;
This brighter sun moves in a boundless sphere;
Of heaven the joy, the glory, and the light,
Shines among angels, and admits no night.

CANTO V

This Iron Age (so fraudulent and bold!)
Touch'd with this love, would be an Age of Gold;
Not, as they feign'd, that oaks should honey drop,
Or land neglected bear an unsown crop;
Love would make all things easy, safe, and cheap;
None for himself would either sow or reap;
Our ready help, and mutual love, would yield
A nobler harvest than the richest field.
Famine and death, confined to certain parts,
Extended are by barrenness of hearts.
Some pine for want where others surfeit now;
But then we should the use of plenty know.
Love would betwixt the rich and needy stand,
And spread heaven's bounty with an equal hand;
At once the givers and receivers bless,
Increase their joy, and make their suff'ring less.
Who for Himself no miracle would make,
Dispensed with sev'ral for the people's sake;
He that, long fasting, would no wonder show,
Made loaves and fishes, as they ate them, grow.
Of all His power, which boundless was above,
Here He used none but to express His love;
And such a love would make our joy exceed,
Not when our own, but other mouths we feed.

Laws would be useless which rude nature awe;
Love, changing nature, would prevent the law;
Tigers and lions into dens we thrust,
But milder creatures with their freedom trust.
Devils are chain'd, and tremble; but the Spouse
No force but love, nor bond but bounty, knows.
Men (whom we now so fierce and dangerous see)
Would guardian angels to each other be;
Such wonders can this mighty love perform,
Vultures to doves, wolves into lambs transform!
Love what Isaiah prophesied can do,[1]
Exalt the valleys, lay the mountains low,
Humble the lofty, the dejected raise,
Smooth and make straight our rough and crooked ways.
Love, strong as death, and like it, levels all;
With that possess'd, the great in title fall;
Themselves esteem but equal to the least,
Whom Heaven with that high character has bless'd.
This love, the centre of our union, can

Alone bestow complete repose on man;
Tame his wild appetite, make inward peace,
And foreign strife among the nations cease.
No martial trumpet should disturb our rest,
Nor princes arm, though to subdue the East,
Where for the tomb so many heroes (taught
By those that guided their devotion) fought.
Thrice happy we, could we like ardour have
To gain His love, as they to win His grave!
Love as He loved! A love so unconfined,
With arms extended, would embrace mankind.
Self-love would cease, or be dilated, when
We should behold as many selfs as men;
All of one family, in blood allied,
His precious blood, that for our ransom died.

FOOTNOTE
[1] 'Prophesied can do': Isaiah xl. 4.

CANTO VI

Though the creation (so divinely taught!)
Prints such a lively image on our thought,
That the first spark of new-created light,
From Chaos struck, affects our present sight:
Yet the first Christians did esteem more bless'd
The day of rising, than the day of rest,
That every week might new occasion give,
To make His triumph in their mem'ry live.
Then let our Muse compose a sacred charm,
To keep His blood among us ever warm,
And singing as the blessed do above,
With our last breath dilate this flame of love.
But on so vast a subject who can find
Words that may reach th'idea of his mind?
Our language fails; or, if it could supply,
What mortal thought can raise itself so high?
Despairing here, we might abandon art,
And only hope to have it in our heart.
But though we find this sacred task too hard,
Yet the design, th'endeavour, brings reward.
The contemplation does suspend our woe,
And makes a truce with all the ills we know.
As Saul's afflicted spirit from the sound
Of David's harp, a present solace found;[1]
So, on this theme while we our Muse engage,

No wounds are felt, of fortune or of age.
On divine love to meditate is peace,
And makes all care of meaner things to cease.

Amazed at once, and comforted, to find
A boundless power so infinitely kind,
The soul contending to that light to flee
From her dark cell, we practise how to die;
Employing thus the poet's winged art,
To reach this love, and grave it in our heart.
Joy so complete, so solid, and severe,
Would leave no place for meaner pleasures there;
Pale they would look, as stars that must be gone,
When from the East the rising sun comes on.

FOOTNOTE
[1] 'Solace found': 1 Sam. xvi. 23.

OF THE FEAR OF GOD. IN TWO CANTOS

CANTO I

The fear of God is freedom, joy, and peace,
And makes all ills that vex us here to cease.
Though the word fear some men may ill endure,
'Tis such a fear as only makes secure.
Ask of no angel to reveal thy fate;
Look in thy heart, the mirror of thy state.
He that invites will not th'invited mock,
Opening to all that do in earnest knock.
Our hopes are all well-grounded on this fear;
All our assurance rolls upon that sphere.
This fear, that drives all other fears away,
Shall be my song, the morning of our day;
Where that fear is, there's nothing to be fear'd;
It brings from heaven an angel for a guard.
Tranquillity and peace this fear does give;
Hell gapes for those that do without it live.
It is a beam, which He on man lets fall,
Of light, by which He made and governs all.
'Tis God alone should not offended be;
But we please others, as more great than He.
For a good cause, the sufferings of man
May well be borne; 'tis more than angels can.
Man, since his fall, in no mean station rests,
Above the angels, or below the beasts.

He with true joy their hearts does only fill,
That thirst and hunger to perform His will.
Others, though rich, shall in this world be vex'd,
And sadly live in terror of the next.
The world's great conqu'ror[1] would his point pursue,
And wept because he could not find a new;
Which had he done, yet still he would have cried,
To make him work until a third he spied.
Ambition, avarice, will nothing owe
To Heaven itself, unless it make them grow.
Though richly fed, man's care does still exceed;
Has but one mouth, yet would a thousand feed.
In wealth and honour, by such men possess'd,
If it increase not, there is found no rest.
All their delight is while their wish comes in;
Sad when it stops, as there had nothing been.
'Tis strange men should neglect their present store,
And take no joy but in pursuing more;
No! though arrived at all the world can aim;
This is the mark and glory of our frame,
A soul capacious of the Deity,
Nothing but He that made can satisfy.
A thousand worlds, if we with Him compare,
Less than so many drops of water are.
Men take no pleasure but in new designs;
And what they hope for, what they have outshines.
Our sheep and oxen seem no more to crave,
With full content feeding on what they have;
Vex not themselves for an increase of store,
But think to-morrow we shall give them more.
What we from day to day receive from Heaven,
They do from us expect it should be given.
We made them not, yet they on us rely,
More than vain men upon the Deity;
More beasts than they! that will not understand
That we are fed from His immediate hand.
Man, that in Him has being, moves, and lives,
What can he have, or use, but what He gives?
So that no bread can nourishment afford,
Or useful be, without His sacred Word.

FOOTNOTE
[1] *'Great conqueror': Alexander.*

CANTO II

Earth praises conquerors for shedding blood,

Heaven those that love their foes, and do them good.
It is terrestrial honour to be crown'd
For strewing men, like rushes, on the ground.
True glory 'tis to rise above them all,
Without th'advantage taken by their fall.
He that in sight diminishes mankind,
Does no addition to his stature find;
But he that does a noble nature show,
Obliging others, still does higher grow;
For virtue practised such a habit gives,
That among men he like an angel lives;
Humbly he doth, and without envy, dwell,
Loved and admired by those he does excel.
Fools anger show, which politicians hide;
Bless'd with this fear, men let it not abide.
The humble man, when he receives a wrong,
Refers revenge to whom it doth belong;
Nor sees he reason why he should engage,
Or vex his spirit for another's rage.
Placed on a rock, vain men he pities, toss'd
On raging waves, and in the tempest lost.
The rolling planets, and the glorious sun,
Still keep that order which they first begun;
They their first lesson constantly repeat,
Which their Creator as a law did set.
Above, below, exactly all obey;
But wretched men have found another way;
Knowledge of good and evil, as at first,
(That vain persuasion!) keeps them still accursed!
The Sacred Word refusing as a guide,
Slaves they become to luxury and pride.
As clocks, remaining in the skilful hand
Of some great master, at the figure stand,
But when abroad, neglected they do go,
At random strike, and the false hour do show;
So from our Maker wandering, we stray,
Like birds that know not to their nests the way.
In Him we dwelt before our exile here,
And may, returning, find contentment there:
True joy may find, perfection of delight,
Behold his face, and shun eternal night.

Silence, my Muse! make not these jewels cheap,
Exposing to the world too large a heap.
Of all we read, the Sacred Writ is best,
Where great truths are in fewest words express'd.

Wrestling with death, these lines I did indite;

No other theme could give my soul delight.
Oh that my youth had thus employ'd my pen!
Or that I now could write as well as then!
But 'tis of grace, if sickness, age, and pain,
Are felt as throes, when we are born again;
Timely they come to wean us from this earth,
As pangs that wait upon a second birth.

OF DIVINE POESY. TWO CANTOS

Occasioned upon sight of the 53d chapter of Isaiah turned into verse by Mrs. Wharton

CANTO I

Poets we prize, when in their verse we find
Some great employment of a worthy mind.
Angels have been inquisitive to know
The secret which this oracle does show.
What was to come, Isaiah did declare,
Which she describes as if she had been there;
Had seen the wounds, which, to the reader's view,
She draws so lively that they bleed anew.
As ivy thrives which on the oak takes hold,
So, with the prophet's, may her lines grow old!
If they should die, who can the world forgive,
(Such pious lines!) when wanton Sappho's live?
Who with His breath His image did inspire,
Expects it should foment a nobler fire;
Not love which brutes as well as men may know,
But love like His, to whom that breath we owe.
Verse so design'd, on that high subject wrote,
Is the perfection of an ardent thought;
The smoke which we from burning incense raise,
When we complete the sacrifice of praise.
In boundless verse the fancy soars too high
For any object but the Deity.
What mortal can with Heaven pretend to share
In the superlatives of wise and fair?
A meaner subject when with these we grace,
A giant's habit on a dwarf we place.
Sacred should be the product of our Muse,
Like that sweet oil, above all private use,
On pain of death forbidden to be made,
But when it should be on the altar laid.
Verse shows a rich inestimable vein

When, dropp'd from heaven, 'tis thither sent again.

Of bounty 'tis that He admits our praise,
Which does not Him, but us that yield it, raise;
For as that angel up to heaven did rise,
Borne on the flame of Manoah's sacrifice,
So, wing'd with praise, we penetrate the sky;
Teach clouds and stars to praise Him as we fly;
The whole creation, (by our fall made groan!)
His praise to echo, and suspend their moan.
For that He reigns, all creatures should rejoice,
And we with songs supply their want of voice.
The church triumphant, and the church below,
In songs of praise their present union show;
Their joys are full; our expectation long;
In life we differ, but we join in song.
Angels and we, assisted by this art,
May sing together, though we dwell apart.
Thus we reach heaven, while vainer poems must
No higher rise than winds may lift the dust.
From that they spring; this from His breath that gave,
To the first dust, th'immortal soul we have;
His praise well sung (our great endeavour here),
Shakes off the dust, and makes that breath appear.

CANTO II

He that did first this way of writing grace,[1]
Conversed with the Almighty face to face;
Wonders he did in sacred verse unfold,
When he had more than eighty winters told.
The writer feels no dire effect of age,
Nor verse, that flows from so divine a rage.
Eldest of Poets, he beheld the light,
When first it triumph'd o'er eternal night;
Chaos he saw, and could distinctly tell
How that confusion into order fell.
As if consulted with, he has express'd
The work of the Creator, and His rest;
How the flood drown'd the first offending race,
Which might the figure of our globe deface.
For new-made earth, so even and so fair,
Less equal now, uncertain makes the air;
Surprised with heat, and unexpected cold,
Early distempers make our youth look old;
Our days so evil, and so few, may tell
That on the ruins of that world we dwell.

Strong as the oaks that nourish'd them, and high,
That long-lived race did on their force rely,
Neglecting Heaven; but we, of shorter date!
Should be more mindful of impendent fate.
To worms, that crawl upon this rubbish here,
This span of life may yet too long appear;
Enough to humble, and to make us great,
If it prepare us for a nobler seat.

Which well observing, he, in numerous lines,
Taught wretched man how fast his life declines;
In whom he dwelt before the world was made,
And may again retire when that shall fade.
The lasting Iliads have not lived so long
As his and Deborah's triumphant song.
Delphos unknown, no Muse could them inspire,
But that which governs the celestial choir.
Heaven to the pious did this art reveal,
And from their store succeeding poets steal.
Homer's Scamander for the Trojans fought,
And swell'd so high, by her old Kishon taught.
His river scarce could fierce Achilles stay;
Hers, more successful, swept her foes away.
The host of heaven, his Phoebus and his Mars,
He arms, instructed by her fighting stars.
She led them all against the common foe;
But he (misled by what he saw below!)
The powers above, like wretched men, divides,
And breaks their union into different sides.
The noblest parts which in his heroes shine,
May be but copies of that heroine.
Homer himself, and Agamemnon, she
The writer could, and the commander, be.
Truth she relates in a sublimer strain,
Than all the tales the boldest Greeks could feign;
For what she sung that Spirit did indite,
Which gave her courage and success in fight.
A double garland crowns the matchless dame;
From heaven her poem and her conquest came.

Though of the Jews she merit most esteem,
Yet here the Christian has the greater theme;
Her martial song describes how Sis'ra fell;
This sings our triumph over death and hell.
The rising light employ'd the sacred breath
Of the blest Virgin and Elizabeth.
In songs of joy the angels sung His birth;
Here how He treated was upon the earth

Trembling we read! th'affliction and the scorn,
Which for our guilt so patiently was borne!
Conception, birth, and suff'ring, all belong
(Though various parts) to one celestial song;
And she, well using so divine an art,
Has in this concert sung the tragic part.

As Hannah's seed was vow'd to sacred use,
So here this lady consecrates her Muse.
With like reward may Heaven her bed adorn,
With fruit as fair as by her Muse is born!

FOOTNOTE

[1] 'Writing grace': Moses.

ON THE PARAPHRASE OF THE LORD'S PRAYER. WRITTEN BY MRS WHARTON

Silence, you winds! listen, ethereal lights!
While our Urania sings what Heaven indites;
The numbers are the nymph's; but from above
Descends the pledge of that eternal love.
Here wretched mortals have not leave alone,
But are instructed to approach His throne;
And how can He to miserable men
Deny requests which His own hand did pen?

In the Evangelists we find the prose
Which, paraphrased by her, a poem grows;
A devout rapture! so divine a hymn,
It may become the highest seraphim!
For they, like her, in that celestial choir,
Sing only what the Spirit does inspire.
Taught by our Lord, and theirs, with us they may
For all but pardon for offences pray.

SOME REFLECTIONS OF HIS UPON THE SEVERAL PETITIONS IN THE SAME PRAYER

I
His sacred name with reverence profound
Should mention'd be, and trembling at the sound!
It was Jehovah; 'tis Our Father now;
So low to us does Heaven vouchsafe to bow![1]
He brought it down that taught us how to pray,
And did so dearly for our ransom pay.

II

His kingdom come. For this we pray in vain
Unless he does in our affections reign.
Absurd it were to wish for such a King,
And not obedience to His sceptre bring,
Whose yoke is easy, and His burthen light,
His service freedom, and his judgments right.

III

His will be done. In fact 'tis always done;
But, as in heaven, it must be made our own.
His will should all our inclinations sway,
Whom Nature, and the universe, obey.
Happy the man! whose wishes are confined
To what has been eternally designed;
Referring all to His paternal care,
To whom more dear than to ourselves we are.

IV

It is not what our avarice hoards up;
'Tis He that feeds us, and that fills our cup;
Like new-born babes depending on the breast,
From day to day we on His bounty feast;
Nor should the soul expect above a day,
To dwell in her frail tenement of clay;
The setting sun should seem to bound our race,
And the new day a gift of special grace.

V

That he should all our trespasses forgive,
While we in hatred with our neighbours live;
Though so to pray may seem an easy task,
We curse ourselves when thus inclined we ask,
This prayer to use, we ought with equal care
Our souls, as to the sacrament, prepare.
The noblest worship of the Power above,
Is to extol, and imitate his love;
Not to forgive our enemies alone,
But use our bounty that they may be won.

VI

Guard us from all temptations of the foe;
And those we may in several stations know;
The rich and poor in slipp'ry places stand.
Give us enough, but with a sparing hand!
Not ill-persuading want, nor wanton wealth,
But what proportion'd is to life and health.

For not the dead, but living, sing thy praise,
Exalt thy kingdom, and thy glory raise.

Favete linguis!...
Virginibus puerisque canto.—HOR.

FOOTNOTE
[1] 'Vouchsafe to bow': Psalm xviii. 9.

ON THE FOREGOING DIVINE POEMS

When we for age could neither read nor write,
The subject made us able to indite;
The soul, with nobler resolutions deck'd,
The body stooping, does herself erect.
No mortal parts are requisite to raise
Her that, unbodied, can her Maker praise.

The seas are quiet when the winds give o'er;
So, calm are we when passions are no more!
For then we know how vain it was to boast
Of fleeting things, so certain to be lost.
Clouds of affection from our younger eyes
Conceal that emptiness which age descries.

The soul's dark cottage, batter'd and decay'd,
Lets in new light through chinks that time has made;
Stronger by weakness, wiser men become,
As they draw near to their eternal home.
Leaving the old, both worlds at once they view,
That stand upon the threshold of the new.

....Miratur limen Olympi.—VIRG.

THE LIFE OF EDMUND WALLER

It is too true, after all, that the lives of poets are not, in general, very interesting. Could we, indeed, trace the private workings of their souls, and read the pages of their mental and moral development, no biographies could be richer in instruction, and even entertainment, than those of our greater bards. The inner life of every true poet must be poetical. But in proportion to the romance of their souls' story, is often the commonplace of their outward career. There have been poets, however, whose lives are quite as readable and as instructive as their poetry, and have even shed a reflex and powerful interest on their writings. The interest of such lives has, in general, proceeded either from the extraordinary misfortunes of the bard, or from his extremely bad morals, or from his strange personal idiosyncrasy, or from his being involved in the political or religious conflicts of his age. The life of Milton, for instance, is rendered intensely interesting from his connexion with the public affairs of his critical and solemn era. The life of Johnson is made readable from his peculiar conformation of body, his bear-like manners, his oddities, and his early struggles. You devour the life of Gifford, not because he was a poet, but because he was a shoemaker; and that of Byron, more on account of his vices, his peerage, and his domestic unhappiness, than for the sake of his poetry. And in Waller, too, you feel some supplemental interest, because he united what are usually thought the incompatible characters of a poet and a political plotter, and very nearly reached the altitudes of the gallows as well as those of Parnassus.

March 1605 was the date, and Coleshill, in Hertfordshire, the place, of the birth of our poet. He was of an ancient and honourable family originally from Kent, some members of which were distinguished for their wealth and others for the valour with which, at Agincourt and elsewhere, they fought the battles of their country. Robert Waller, the poet's father, inherited from Edmund, his father, the lands of Beaconsfield, in Bucks, and other territory in Hertfordshire. These had been in 1548-9 left by Francis Waller, in default of issue by his own wife, to his brothers Thomas and Edmund, but Thomas dying, Edmund inherited the whole. Robert, on receiving his estates, quitted the profession of the law, to which he had attached himself, and spent the rest of his life chiefly at Beaconsfield, employed in the manly business and healthy amusements of a country gentleman. He died in August 1616, and left a widow and a son—the son, Edmund, being eleven years of age. It was at Beaconsfield. We need hardly remind our readers, that a far greater Edmund—Edmund Burke—spent many of his days. It was there that he composed his latest and noblest works, the "Reflections on the French Revolution," and the "Letters on a Regicide Peace;" and there he surrendered to the Creator one of the subtlest, strongest, brightest, and best of human souls. Shortly after Burke's death, the house of Beaconsfield was burnt down, and no trace of it is now, we believe, extant.

Mrs. Waller's brother, William, was the father of John Hampden. His wife, Elizabeth Cromwell, the aunt of the great Oliver, was, however, and continued to the end, a violent Royalist; and Cromwell, although he treated both her and her son with kindness, and on the terms of their relationship, was so provoked at hearing that she carried on a secret correspondence with the Stewart party, that he confined her under a very strict watch in the house of her daughter, Mrs. Price, whose husband was on the side of the Parliament. It is exceedingly probable that from the "mother's milk" of early prejudice was derived that spirit of partisanship which distinguished alike the writings and the life of the poet. It is possible, too, that contact with men so far above moral heroism and rugged mental force as Cromwell and Hampden, instead of exciting emulation, led to envy, and that his divergence from their political path sprung more from personal feeling than from principle.

He was educated, first, at the grammar school of Market, Wickham; then at Eton; and, in fine, at King's College, Cambridge. Accounts vary as to his proficiency—one Bigge, who had been his school-fellow at Wickham, told Aubrey that he never expected Waller to have become such an eminent poet, and that he used to write his exercises for him. Others, on the contrary, have alleged that it was the fame of his scholarship which led to his election for Agmondesham, a borough in Bucks, when he was only sixteen years of age. This story, so far as his premature learning goes, seems rather apocryphal; but certain it is, that when scarcely eighteen, he had become M.P. for the above-mentioned borough. The parliament in which he found himself, was one of those subservient and cringing assemblies which James I. was wont to summon to sit till they had voted the supplies, and then contemptuously to dismiss. It met in November 1621, and after passing a resolution in support of their privileges, which James tore out of the Journals with his own hand, and granting the usual supplies, was dissolved on the 6th of January 1622. Waller was probably as silent and servile as any of his neighbours. He began, however, to feel his way as a courtier, and overheard some curious and not very canonical talk of James with his lords and bishops, the record of which reminds you of some of the richer scenes of the "Fortunes of Nigel." The next parliament was not called till 1624, when Waller was not elected. The electors of Agmondesham, who had, meantime, obtained fuller privileges, chose two matured members to represent them, and the precocious boy lost his seat.

Waller's "political and poetical life began nearly together." It was in his eighteenth year that he wrote his first poetical piece—that on the escape of Prince Charles from a tempest on his return from Spain. It is a tissue of smooth and musical mediocrity. It shews a kind of stunted prematurity. The perfection which is attained by a single effort is generally a poor and tame one. This poem of Waller's, like several of his others, has all that merit which arises from the absence of fault, and all that fault which arises from the absence of merit—of high poetic merit, we mean, for in music it is equal to any of his poems. Much has been said about the model which he followed in his versification, the majority of critics tracing in it an imitation of Fairfax's Tasso. The fact seems to be that Waller, with a good ear, had a very limited theory of verse. He worshipped smoothness, and sought it at every hazard. He preferred the Jacob of a soft flowing commonplace to the rough hairy Esau of a strong originality, cumbered with its own weight and richness. We think that this excessive love of the soft, and horror at the rude, materially weakened his genius. The true theory of versification lies in variety, and in accommodation to the necessities and fluctuations of the thought. The "Paradise Lost," written in Waller's rhyme, would have been as ridiculous as Waller's love to Saccharissa expressed in Milton's blank verse. The school before Waller were too rugged, but surely there is a medium between the roughness of Donne, and the honied monotony of the author of the "Summer Islands." The practice of running the lines into one another, severely condemned by Johnson, and systematically shunned by Waller, has often been practised with success by poets far greater than either—such as Shelley and Coleridge. It is remarkable that Dryden, while he praised, did not copy our poet's manner, but gave himself freer scope. Pope, on the other hand, pushed his love of uniform tinkle and unmitigated softness to excess, and transferred this kind of luscious verse from small poems, where it is often a merit, to large ones, where it is a mistake. In his "Iliad," for instance, the fierce ire of Achilles, the dignified resentment of Agamemnon, the dull courage of Ajax, the chivalrous sentiment of Hector, the glowing energy of Diomede, the veteran wisdom of Nestor, the grief of Andromache, the love of Helen, the jealousy of Juno, and the godlike majesty of Jupiter, are all expressed in the same sweet and monotonous melody—a verse called "heroic," by courtesy, or on the principle of contradiction, like lucus a non lucendo. In Waller, however, his poems being all, without exception, rather short, you never think of quarrelling with his uniformity of manner; and rise from his lines as from a liberal feast of hot-house grapes, thankful, but feeling that a few more would have turned satisfaction into nausea. Yet you feel, too, that perhaps his selection of small themes, and the consequent curbing of his powers, have sprung from his fastidiousness in the matter of versification. The sermons, the satires, the speeches, the odes, and the didactic poems of the fastidious are generally short, and do not, therefore, fully mirror the amplitude, or express the energy of their genius. To his poem on the escape of Prince Charles, succeeded that on the Prince, and two or three others of a similar kind; all finding their inspiration, not as yet in that love of others which animated his amatory effusions, but in that love to himself and his own interest which marks the incipient courtier, who is beginning, in Shakspeare's thought, to hang his knee upon "hinges," that it may bend more readily to power. Yet his case shews that there is a certain incompatibility between the profession of a courtier and that of a poet. He often began his panegyrics with much fervour, but the fit passed, or his fastidious taste produced disgust at what he had written, and it was either not finished, or was delayed till the interest of the occasion had passed away.

After the death of James I., Charles called a new parliament in 1625, and in it Waller took his place for Chipping-Wycombe, a borough in Buckinghamshire. This parliament met in London, but was adjourned to Oxford on account of the Plague. In Oxford, it proved refractory to the king's wishes, and refusing to grant him a tithe of the supplies which he demanded, was summarily dismissed. Waller was not re-elected in 1626, when the next parliament was summoned, but secured his return for Agmondesham in March 1627. He appears to have been in these years a silent senator, taking little interest or share in the debates, but retiring from them to offer the quit-rent of his versicles—a laureate without salary, and yet not probably much more sincere than laureates generally are; for although his loyalty was undoubted, his expressions of it in rhyme are often hyperbolical to a degree.

In his twenty-sixth year, he married an heiress, the daughter of Mr. Banks, a wealthy London citizen. In this there was nothing singular but the fact, that he, as yet obscure, distanced a rival of great influence, whose suit was supported by royalty—namely, Mr. Crofts, afterwards Baron Crofts—gave rather a romantic and adventurous air to the match. He retired soon after to Beaconsfield, where he spent some happy years in the enjoyment of domestic society, pursuing, too, his studies under the direction of Morley, afterwards Bishop of Winchester, a distinguished scholar of the time, who resided with him. During this period he is said to have read many poets, but to have written little poetry. Although the king, jealous of his subjects, had, in 1632, by a most absurd and arbitrary decree, commanded all the lords and gentry in the kingdom to reside on their own estates, Waller did not at the time consider this an exceeding hardship. Indeed, his feelings were on no subject, and under no pressure of circumstances, either very profound or very lasting.

His wife died after having borne him a son and a daughter—a son, who did not long survive his mother; and a daughter, who became afterwards Mrs. Dormer of Oxfordshire. From under this calamity Waller, yet only thirty years of age, rebounded with characteristic elasticity. He came back, nothing both, to the society he had left, and was soon known to be in quest of a fair lady, whom he has made immortal by the sobriquet of Saccharissa. She was the eldest daughter of the Earl of Leicester, and her name was the Lady Dorothy Sidney. This lady was counted beautiful. Her father was absent in foreign parts. She lived almost alone in Penshurst. It added to her charms, at least in a poetical eye, that she was descended from Sir Philip Sidney; a man whose name, as the flower of chivalry and the soul of honour, is still "like ointment poured forth" in the estimation of the world—whose death rises almost to the dignity and grandeur of a martyrdom—and who has left in his "Arcadia" a quaintly decorated, conceived, and unequally chiselled, but true, rich, and magnificent monument of his genius. In spite, however, of all Waller's tender ditties, of the incense he offered up—not only to Dorothy, but to her sister Lady Lucy, and even to her maid Mrs. Braughton—his goddess was inexorable, and not only rejected, but spurned him from her feet. The poet bore this disappointment, as all poets, Dante hardly excepted, have borne the same: he transferred his affections to another, who, indeed, ere Saccharissa-like the sun had set in the west, had risen like the moon in the east of her lover's admiration, and soon, although only for a short time, possessed the sky alone. This was his Amoret, who is said to have been Lady Sophia Murray. The Juliet, however, was not one whit more placable than the Rosalind— she, too, rejected his suit; and this rejection threw Waller, not into despair or melancholy, but into a wide sea of miscellaneous flirtations, with we know not how many Chlorises, Sylvias, Phyllises, and Flavias, all which names stood, it seems, for real persons, and testified to a universality in the poet's affections which is rather ludicrous than edifying. His heart was as soft, and shallower than his verse.

Saccharissa married Lord Spencer, afterwards the Earl of Sunderland, who was killed at the battle of Newbury. After his death, she was united to a Mr. Robert Smythe; and she now lies at Brinton, in Northamptonshire, while her picture continues, from the walls of the gallery at Penshurst, to shed down the soft, languishing, and voluptuous smile which had captivated the passions, if it could hardly be said to have really touched the heart, of her poetical admirer. He not very long after his twofold rejection, consoled himself by marrying a second wife. Her name was Breaux or Bresse; and all we know of her is, that she bore and brought up a great many children.

In 1639, the urgencies of the times compelled Charles to call a new parliament, and it was decreed that politics instead of love and song should now for a time engross our poet. And there opened up to him unquestionably a noble field of patriotic exertion had he been fully adapted for its cultivation—his firmness been equal to his eloquence, and his sincerity to his address—had he been more of a Whig in the good old Hampden sense, and less of a trimmer. As it is, he cuts, on the whole, a doubtful figure, and is no great favourite with the partisans of either of the great contending parties. He was again elected member for Agmondesham, and when the question came before the House, whether the supplies demanded by Strafford should be granted, or the grievances complained of by the Commons should be first redressed, he delivered an oration, trying with considerable dexterity to steer a medium course between the two sides. In this speech, while contending for the constitutional principle advocated by the Commons, and expressing great attachment to his Majesty's person, he maintained that the chief blame of the king's obnoxious measures lay with his clerical advisers, and concluded by moving that the House should first consider the grievances, and then grant the royal demand. Charles, who had personally requested Waller to second the motion for instantly granting the supplies, was not, we imagine, particularly pleased with his "volunteer" laureate's conduct; and his temporary defection did not tend to allay the royal fury at the parliament, which burst out forthwith in an act of sudden and wrathful dismissal.

This session, called from its extreme brevity the Short Parliament, ended in May. In November met that memorable assembly, destined not to separate till it had outlived a monarchy and a hierarchy, and seen a brewer's son take the sceptre instead of the descendant of a hundred kings, the Long Parliament. Waller, again member for Agmondesham, had made himself popular by his speech in the beginning of the year, and was chosen by the Commons to manage the prosecution of Judge Crawley for advising the levy of ship-money. He conducted the case with talent, acuteness, and moderation. Soon after, however, as the gulph widened between the king and the parliament, his position became extremely awkward. His understanding on the whole was with the parliament, although he did not approve of some of their measures, but his heart was with the royal cause. He first of all, along with a others (whose example was imitated by Fox and his party during the French Revolution), retired from parliament, but in consequence of the permission or request of the king, he speedily resumed his seat. When Charles put himself in a warlike attitude in August 1642, Waller sent him a present of a thousand broad pieces. Still his plausible language, the tone of moderation which he preserved, and his connexion with Cromwell and Hampden, rendered the popular party unwilling to believe him a traitor to their cause, and he was appointed, after the battle at Edgehill, one of the commissioners who met at Oxford to treat of peace. Here, it is said, that one of those compliments which cost the subtle Charles so little (Waller was last in being presented to the king, and his Majesty told him, "Though last, you are not the lowest nor the least in my favour"), gained over Waller, and suggested to him the scheme of his famous plot. We do not think so little of our hero's intellect, or so much of his heart, as to credit this story. Though not aged, he was by far too old to be caught with such chaff. He knew, too, before, Charles' private sentiments towards him, and we incline with some of his biographers to suppose that these words of royalty were simply the signal to Waller to fire the train which the king knew right well had already been prepared.

Poets are in general poor politicians and miserable plotters. They seldom, even in verse or fiction, manage a state plot well. Scott, at least, has completely failed in his treatment of the Popish plot in "Peveril," and they always bungle it in reality. They are either too unsuspicious or too scheming, too shallow or too profound. That mixture of transparency and craft, of simplicity and subtlety, requisite to all deep schemes, and which Poe (himself a confused compound of the genius, the simpleton, and the scoundrel) has so admirably exemplified in the "Purloined Letter," is not often competent to men of imagination and impulse. Waller was not a very creative spirit; but here he was true to his class, and failed like a very poet. He had a brother-in-law named Tomkins, clerk of the Queen's Council, and possessed of much influence in the city. Consulting together on national affairs, it struck them simultaneously that energetic measures might yet save the court. They saw, or thought they saw, a reaction in favour of the royal cause, and they determined to try and unite the royalists together in a peaceful but strong combination against the parliament. They appointed confidential agents to make out, in the different parishes and wards, lists of those persons who were or were not friendly to their cause; and to secure secrecy, they prohibited more than three of their party from meeting in one place, and no individual was to reveal the design to more than two others. Lord Conway, fresh from Ireland, joined the confederacy, and probably the counsels of such an ardent soldier served to modify the original purpose, and to give it a military colour. Meanwhile, Sir Nicholas Crispe, a bolder spirit than Waller, had organised a different scheme in favour of Charles. He had, when a merchant in the city, procured a loan of £100,000 for the king; he had then raised and taken the command of a regiment; he had obtained from Charles a commission of array, which Lady Aubigny, ignorant of its contents, was to deliver to a gentleman in London. Crispe's plan was bold and comprehensive. He intended to remove the king's children to a place of safety, to enlist soldiers, collect magazines, and raise monies by contribution, to release the prisoners committed by the parliament, to arrest some of the leading members in both Houses, to issue declarations, and whenever the conspiracy was ripe, to raise flags at Temple Bar, the Exchange, and other central spots.

It was impossible that two such plots could escape collision with each other—or that either should be long concealed. On the 31st May 1643, a fast-day, Pym is seated in St. Margaret's Church, hearing sermon. A messenger enters and gives him a letter. He reads hastily—communicates its intelligence in whispers to those beside him, and hurries out. No time is lost. Pym and his party could not trifle now though they would, and would not though they could. Waller and Tomkins are seized that night in their houses, and overwhelmed with fear, confess everything. It is suspected that Waller was betrayed by his sister, Mrs. Price, who was married to a zealous parliamentarian. A strange story is told, that one Goode, her chaplain, had stolen some of his papers, and would have got a hold of them all, had not Waller, having DREAMED that his sister was perfidious, risen and secured the rest. Clarendon, on the other hand, says that the discovery was made by a servant of Tomkins, who acted as a spy for the parliament. At all events, they were found out, and, in their terror and pusillanimity, they betrayed their associates. The Duke of Portland and Lord Conway were instantly arrested. Lady Aubigny, too, was imprisoned, but contrived to make her escape to the Hague. Even the Earl of Northumberland was involved in the charges which now issued in a trembling torrent from the lips of the detected conspirator, who confessed a great deal that could not have been discovered, and offered to reveal the private conversations of ladies of rank, and to betray all and sundry who were in the slightest degree connected with the plot. Tomkins had somehow got possession of Crispe's commission of array, which he had buried in the garden, but which was now, on his information, dug up. Never did a conspiracy fall to pieces more rapidly, completely, and, for the conspirators, more disgracefully.

This discovery proves a windfall to the parliamentary party. Pym hies to the citizens and apprises them, in one breath, at once of their danger and their signal deliverance. The Commons draw up a vow and covenant, expressing their detestation of all such conspiracies, and appoint a day of thanksgiving for the escape of the nation. Meanwhile Waller and Portland are confronted, when the one repeats his charge and Portland denies it. Conway, too, maintains his innocence, and as Waller is the only evidence against either him or Portland, both are, after a long imprisonment, admitted to bail. Tomkins, Chaloner (the agent of Crispe), Hassel (the king's courier between Oxford and London), Alexander Hampden (Waller's cousin), and some subordinate conspirators, are arraigned before a Council of War. Waller feigns himself so ill with remorse of conscience, that his trial is put off that he "may recover his understanding." Hassel dies the night before the trial. Tomkins and Chaloner are hanged before their own doors. Hampden escapes punishment, but is retained in prison, where he dies; and the subordinates just referred to (Blinkorne and White) are pardoned. Northumberland, owing to his rank, is only once examined before the Lords. Those whose names were inserted in the commission of array are treated as malignants, and their estates seized.

Waller, having received some respite, employed the time in petitioning, flattering, bribing, confessing, beseeching, and in the exercise of every other art by which a mean, cowardly spirit seeks to evade death. He appealed from the military jurisdiction to the House of Commons, and was admitted to plead his cause at their bar. His speech was humble, conciliating, and artful, but failed to gain the object. He was expelled from the House, and soon after was sisted before the Court of War, and condemned to die. He was reprieved, however, by Essex, and at the end of a year's imprisonment, the sentence was commuted into a fine of £10,000, and banishment for life. He was sent to "recollect himself in another country." He had previously expended, it is said, £30,000 in bribes.

Waller's conduct in this whole matter was a mixture of cowardice and meanness. Recollecting his poetical temperament, and the well-known stories of Demosthenes at Cheronea, and Horace at Philippi, we are not disposed to be harsh on his cowardice, but we have no excuse for his meanness. It discovers a want of heart, and an infinite littleness of soul. We can hardly conceive him to have possessed a drop of the blood of Hampden or Cromwell in his veins, and cease to wonder why two high-spirited ladies of rank should have spurned the homage of a poetic poltroon, whom instinctively they seem to have known to be such, even before he proved it to the world.

"Infamous, and not contented," Waller repairs to the Continent, first to Rouen, then to Switzerland and Italy, in company with his friend Evelyn, and, in fine, settles for a season in Paris. Here he keeps open table for the banished royalists, as well as for the French wits, till his means are impaired by his liberality. A middling poet, a pitiful politician, a fickle dangler in affairs of love, Waller was an admirable host, and not only gave good dinners and suppers, but flavoured them delicately with compliment and repartee. In Paris he recovered his tone of spirits, and, had his money lasted, might have remained there till his dying day. But fines and bribes had exhausted his patrimony, and he was compelled first to sell a property in Bedfordshire, worth more than £1,000 a-year, then to part with his wife's jewels, and in fine to sell the last of these, which he called "the rump jewel." His family, too, had increased, and added to his incumbrances. His favourite was a daughter, Margaret, born in Rouen, who acted as his amanuensis. At last, through the intercession of his brother-in-law, Scroope, he was permitted to return to England. This was on the 13th of January 1652. During all his residence on the Continent, he had continued to amuse himself with poetry, "in which," says Johnson, "he sometimes speaks of the rebels and their usurpation, in the natural language of an honest man." If this mean that Waller, when he uttered such sentiments, was, for the nonce, sincere, it is quite true; but if the Doctor means that Waller was, speaking generally, an honest man, it is not true; and Dr. Johnson repeatedly signifies, in other parts of his life, that he does not believe it to be true. He speaks, for instance, of the "exorbitance of his adulation," of his "having lost the esteem of all parties," and says, "It is not possible to read without some contempt and indignation, poems ascribing the highest degree of power and piety to Charles the First, and then transferring the same power and piety to Oliver Cromwell." In keeping with this, Bishop Burnet asserts, that "in the House he was only concerned to say what should make him applauded, and never laid the business of the House to heart."

Waller, returning, found his mother still alive at Beaconsfield, where Cromwell sometimes visited her; and when she talked in favour of the royal cause, would throw napkins at her, and say that he would not dispute with his aunt, although afterwards, as we have seen, her spirit of political intrigue compelled him to make her a prisoner in her own house. The poet took up his residence near her at Hall-barn, a house of his own erection, and on the walls of which he hung up a picture of Saccharissa, whence he hoped, it may be, draw consolation for the past, and inspiration for the future. Here Cromwell, who probably despised Waller in his heart, as often men of action despise men of mere literary ability, especially when that ability is not transcendent, but whose cue it was to conciliate all men according to their respective positions and capabilities, paid great attention to his kinsman. Waller found Cromwell well acquainted with the ancient historians, and they conversed a good deal on such topics. It is said, that when Waller jeered him on his using the peculiar phraseology of the Puritans in his conversation with them, the Protector answered, "Cousin Waller, I must talk to these men in their own way;" an anecdote which is sometimes quoted as if it proved that Cromwell had no religion; whereas it only proved that he had at heart no cant. It was not as if he had privately avowed infidelity to his kinsman. Cromwell found cant prevalent on his stage, just as any great actor of that century found rant on his, and, like the actor, he used it occasionally as a means of gaining his own lofty ends, and as a foil to his own genuine earnestness and power.

The Protector, however, seems to have profoundly impressed even Waller's light and fickle mind; and the panegyric which he produced on him in 1654, is not only the ablest, but seems the sincerest of his productions. He had hitherto been writing about women, courtiers, and kings; but now he had to gird up his loins and write on a man. The piece is accordingly as masculine in style, as it is just in appreciation; and, with the exception of Milton's glorious sketch in the "Defensio pro populo Anglicano," and Carlyle's lecture in his "Heroes and Hero-worship," it is, perhaps, the best encomium ever pronounced on the Lord Protector of England—almost worthy of Cromwell's unrivalled merits and achievements, and more than worthy of Waller's powers. It is said, that when twitted with having written a better panegyric on Cromwell than a congratulation to Charles II., he wittily replied, "You should remember that poets succeed better in fiction than in truth." Perhaps In this he spoke ironically; certainly the fact was the reverse of his words. It is because he has spoken truth in the first, and fiction in the second, of productions, that the first is incomparably the better poem. Sketches of character taken from the life are better than those where imagination operates on hearsays and on recorded actions. And certainly few men had a better opportunity than Waller of seeing in private and in undress, and with an eye in which native sagacity was sharpened by prejudices, partly for, partly against, the Man of that century—a man in whom we recognise a union of Roman, Hebrew, and English qualities—the faith of the Jew, the firmness of the Roman, and the homespun simplicity of the Englishman of his own age—in purpose and in powers "an armed angel on a battle-day;" in manners a plain blunt corporal; and in language always a stammerer, and sometimes a buffoon; the middle-class man of his time, with the merits and the defects of his order, but touched with an inspiration as from heaven, lifting him far above all the aristocracy, and all the royalty, and all the literature of his period; who found his one great faculty—inflamed and consecrated commonsense—to be more than equal to the subteties, and brilliancies, and wit, and eloquence, and taste, and genius, of his thousand opponents—whose crown was a branch of English oak, his sceptre a strong sapling of the same, his throne a mound of turf—who economised matters by being at once king and king's jester, and whose mere clenched fist, held up at home or across the waters, saved millions of money, awed despots, encouraged freedom in every part of the world, and had nearly established a pure form of Christianity over Great Britain—who gave his country a model of excellence as a man, and as a ruler, simple, severe, ruggedly picturesque, and stupendously original, and solitary as one of the primitive rocks—whose eloquence was uneven and piercing as the forked lightning, which is never so terrible as when it falls to pieces—and highest praise of all, whose deeds and character were so great in their sublime simplicity, that the poet, who afterwards sung the hierarchies of heaven, and the anarchies of hell, was fain to sit a humble secretary, recording the thoughts and actions of Cromwell, and felt afterwards that he had been as nobly employed when defending his grand defiance of evil and arbitrary power, as when he did

"Assert Eternal Providence,
And justify the ways of God to man."

We have seen pictured representations of Cromwell and Milton seated together at the council-table, in which the painter wished more than to insinuate that Milton was the superior being; but in our judgment the advantage was on the other side, and the poet seemed to bear only that relation and proportion to the Protector which the eloquent Raphael, the "affable archangel," the bard of the war in heaven, does to the Gabriel or the Michael, whose tremendous sword mingled in and all but decided the fray. And we thought what a junction were that of the two powers—of the sword and the pen, the actor and the recorder, the man to do, and the poet to sing! Waller in his panegyric sees and shews in a few lines Cromwell's relation to Britain, and that of both to the world:—

"Heaven that has placed this island to give law,
To balance Europe, and her states to awe,
In this conjunction does on Britain smile,
The greatest leader and the greatest isle."

He saw that in Cromwell, and in Cromwell alone, had the power of Britain come to a point: IT was made, if not to be the governor to be the moderator of the earth, and HE was sent to govern it, to condense its scattered energies, to awe down its warring factions, and to wield all its forces to one good and great end. In him for the first time had the wild island, the Bucephalus of the West, found a rider able, by backing, bridling, and curbing him, to give due direction and momentum to his fury, force, and speed.

He has scattered some other precious particles of thought in this poem, such as:—

"Lords of the world's great waste, the ocean, we
Whole forests send to reign upon the sea."

"The Caledonians, arm'd with want and cold."

"The states, changed by you,
Changed like the world's great scene, when without noise,
The rising sun night's vulgar lights destroys."

"Illustrious acts high raptures do infuse,
And every conqueror creates a Muse."

When Cromwell died, Waller again lifted up his pen, and indited a short lamentation over his loss. After the Restoration, he was one of the first to read a poetical recantation of his errors in verses addressed to Charles II. In 1661 he was returned to parliament for Hastings, in Sussex, and sat afterwards at various times for Chipping-Wycombe, and Saltash. In parliament, he was rather famed for his lively sallies of wit, than for his logic, sense, or earnestness. In private, his spirits, even without the aid of wine,—which he never drank,—continued to a great age unusually buoyant. As he advanced in life he became more religious, and intermixed a vein of devotion with his verse. When eighty-two, he bought a small estate in Coleshill, near his native place, desirous, he said, "to die, like the stag, where he was roused." His wish, however, was not granted. Seized with tumours in his legs, he went to Windsor to consult Sir Charles Scarborough, then waiting on the king. Sir Charles, at Waller's request to know the "meaning" of these swellings, told him that they showed that his "blood would no longer run." On this the poet quietly repeated a passage from Virgil, and returned to Beaconsfield to die. Having received the sacrament, and shared it with his children, and expressed his faith in Christianity, he expired on the 21st of October 1687. He was buried in the churchyard of Beaconsfield. He left five sons and eight daughters. His eldest son being an imbecile, Edmund, his second, inherited the estates, and having joined the party of the Prince of Orange, sat for Agmondesham for some years, but became ultimately a Quaker. The fortunes of the rest of his family are not particularly interesting, and need not be related.

As a character, our opinion of Waller has been already indicated. He was indecisive, vacillating, with more wit than judgment, and with more judgment than earnestness. In that age of high hearts, stormy passions, and determined purpose, he looks helpless and not at home, like a butterfly in an eagle's eyrie. A gifted, accomplished, and apparently an amiable man, he was a feeble, and almost a despicable character. The parliament seem to have thought him hardly worth hanging. Cromwell bore with him only as a kinsman, and respected him only as a scholar. Charles II. liked to laugh at his jokes, and to Saville his company was as good as an additional bottle of wine. His only chance of fame as a man of action arose from his connexion with the plot, which, however, in its issue covered him with infamy, as all bad things bungled, inevitably do to those who attempt them.

Although he unquestionably in some points improved our correctness of style and our versification, there is not much to be said either for or against his poetry. It is as a whole a mass of smooth and easy, yet systematic, trifling. Nine-tenths of it does not rise above mediocrity, and the tenth that remains is more distinguished by grace than by grandeur or depth. His lines on Cromwell we have already characterised. It may seem odd, but in his verses on the head of a stag, which Johnson singles out as bad, we see more of the soul of poetry than in any of his other productions.

Let our readers, if they will not be convinced by our assertion, listen to some of these lines:—

"So we some antique hero's strength,
Learn by his lance's weight and length—
As these vast beams express the beast
Whose shady brows alive they dress'd.
Such game, while yet the world was new,
The mighty Nimrod did pursue;
What huntsman of our feeble race
Or dogs dare such a monster chase?
*　　*　　*　　*　　*

Oh, fertile head, which every year
Could such a CROP of WONDER bear!"

In his amorous and complimentary ditties, he is often very successful. So, too, is he in much of his "Divine Poetry," particularly the lines at the end, beginning with—

"The soul's dark cottage, batter'd and decay'd,"
Lets in new light through chinks which time hath made.

These contain a thought, so far as we remember, new and highly poetical.

We may close by saying a few words on a question which Dr. Johnson has started in his "Life of Waller" in reference to sacred poetry. That great and good man, our readers remember, maintains that the ideas of the Christian theology are too simple for eloquence, too sacred for fiction, and too majestic for ornament, and "that faith, thanksgiving, repentance, and supplication," are all unsusceptible of poetical treatment. He grants that the doctrines of religion may be defended in a didactic poem, and that a poet may not only describe God's works in nature, but may trace them up to nature's God. But he asserts that "contemplative piety, or the intercourse between God and the human soul, cannot be poetical." It is curious to remember that, up to Johnson's time, the best poetry in the world had been sacred. There had been the poetry of the Bible, in which truth of the deepest import was expressed, now in "eloquence," now in "fiction," and now in language most gorgeously "ornamented," and in which "Faith" in Isaiah, "Thanksgiving" in Moses, "Penitence" in David, and "Supplication" in Jeremiah, had uttered themselves in sublime, or lively, or subdued, or tender strains —the poetry of the "Divine Commedia," of the "Jerusalem Delivered," of the "Faery Queen," of the "Paradise Lost" and "Paradise Regained," of the "Night-Thoughts," of "Smart's David," all poetry, let it be observed, not defending religion merely, or confining itself to the praise of God's lower works, but entering into the depths of divine contemplation, into the very adyta of the heavenly temple. And it is no less interesting to recollect that in spite of Dr. Johnson's sage diction, sacred poetry of a very high order has, since his day, abounded. Cowper has extracted it from "the intercourse between God and the human soul;" Montgomery has made now "the supplication," and now the "thanksgiving," of the poor negro ring in every ear, and vibrate through every heart; Coleridge has expressed, in his sounding and splendid measures, at one time his "faith," and at another his "repentance;" Pollok has with true, although unequal steps, followed Milton and Dante, both into the heaven of heavens, and into the gloom of Gehenna; and Wordsworth, Southey, Croly, Milman, Trench, Keble, and a host more have, by their noble religious hymns, shamed the wisdom of the Sadducee, and darkened the glory of the song of the sceptic. Why argue about principles while we can appeal to facts? Why shew either the probabilities against, or the probabilities for, good sacred poetry, while we see it before us, gushing from a thousand springs, and gladdening every corner of the church and of the world?

Dr. Johnson says, "Whatever is great, desirable, or tremendous, is comprised in the name of the Supreme Being. Omnipotence cannot be exalted. Infinity cannot be amplified. Perfection cannot be improved." All this is as true as it is pointedly expressed; but though true, it is nothing to the purpose— nay, bears as much against prayer as against poetry. What meant the Psalmist when he said, "My soul doth magnify the Lord?" Did he aspire to exalt Omnipotence or to amplify perfection? No; but only first to shew his own feeling of their magnitude; and, again, to raise himself a step toward an approximately adequate conception of the Most High. So in religious poetry. We cannot add to, or exalt God, but we can raise ourselves up nearer to Him, and attain, if not a full understanding, a deeper feeling of the elements of His surpassing excellence and glory. Indeed, as the highest poetry (in Milton, for instance) blossoms into prayer, so the truest prayer, often by insensible gradation, becomes poetry.

Dr. Johnson says, that "of sentiments purely religious, the most simple expression is the most sublime." True, and hence, the best religious poetry is at once sublime and simple. He adds, "Poetry loses its lustre and its power, because it is applied to the decoration of something more excellent than itself." On this principle, poets should never sing of God's works in nature—of the ocean, or the sun, or the stars—no, nor of the heroic achievements of man's courage, or of the self-sacrifices of his love—for are not all these more excellent than poetry? Dr Johnson's theory would hush the "New Song" itself, and perpetuate that silence which was once in heaven "for half-an-hour."

Long before the Doctor vented this paradox, Cowley, in his preface to his poems, had written the following eloquent and memorable sentences on this subject:—"When I consider how many bright and magnificent subjects Scripture affords, and proffers, as it were, to poesy, in the wise managing and illustrating whereof the glory of God Almighty might be joined with the singular utility and noblest delight of mankind, it is not without grief and indignation that I behold that divine science employing all her inexhaustible riches of wit and eloquence, either in the wicked and beggarly flattering of great persons, or the unmanly idolising of foolish women, or the wretched affectation of scurril laughter, or the confused dreams of senseless fables and metamorphoses. Amongst all holy and consecrated things which the devil ever stole and alienated from the service of the Deity—as altars, temples, sacrifices, prayers, and the like—there is none that he so universally and so long usurped as poetry. It is time to recover it out of the tyrant's hands, and to restore it to the kingdom of God, who is the Father of it. It is time to baptize it in Jordan, for it will never become clean by bathing in the waters of Damascus.

"What can we imagine more proper for the ornaments of wit and learning in the story of Deucalion than in that of Noah? Why will not the actions of Samson afford as plentiful matter as the Labours of Hercules? (Perhaps from this Milton took the hint of writing his "Samson Agonistes.") Why is not Jephtha's daughter as good a woman as Iphigenia? and the friendship of David and Jonathan more worthy celebration than that of Theseus and Pirithous? Does not the passage of Moses and the Israelites into the Holy Land yield incomparably more poetic variety than the voyages of Ulysses and Aeneas? Are the obsolete, threadbare tales of Thebes and Troy half so well stored with great, heroical, and supernatural actions (since verse will needs find or make such), as the wars of Joshua, of the Judges, of David, and divers others? Can all the transformations of the gods give such copious hints to flourish and expatiate on as the true miracles of Christ, or of His prophets and apostles? What do I instance in these few particulars? All the books in the Bible are either already most admirable and exalted pieces of poetry, or are the best materials in the world for it.

"Yet," he adds with great judiciousness, "though they be so proper in themselves to be made use of for this purpose, none but a good artist will know how to do it, neither must we think to cut and polish diamonds with so little pains and skill as we do marble. He who can write a profane poem well, may write a divine one better; but he who can do that but ill, will do this much worse, and so far from elevating poesy will but abase divinity. The same fertility of invention—the same wisdom of disposition—the same judgment in observance of decencies—the same lustre and vigour of elocution— the same modesty and majesty of number— briefly, the same kind of habit—is required in both, only this latter allows better stuff, and therefore would look more deformedly drest in it."

The errors of a great author are often more valuable than his sound sentiments; because they tend, by the reaction they provoke, and the replies they elicit, to dart new light upon the opposite truths. And so it has been with this dogma of the illustrious Lexicographer. It has led to some admirable rejoinders from such pens as those of Montgomery, and of Christopher North, which have not only rebutted

Johnson's objections, but have directed public attention more strongly to the general theme, and served to shed new light upon the nature and province of religious poetry.

www.ingramcontent.com/pod-product-compliance
Lightning Source LLC
Chambersburg PA
CBHW060136050426
42448CB00010B/2161